APPRENTICESHIPS

Business

Customer Service Practitioner

Handbook

LEVEL 2

Elizabeth Blaikie

Lambert Stewart

Sue Tissiman

Pearson

Published by Pearson Education Limited, 80 Strand, London, WC2R 0RL.

www.pearsonschoolsandfecolleges.co.uk

Copies of official specifications for all Pearson qualifications may be found on the website: qualifications.pearson.com

Typeset by PDQ Media

Picture research by Integra

First published 2018

21 20 19 18
10 9 8 7 6 5 4 3 2 1

British Library Cataloguing in Publication Data
A catalogue record for this book is available from the British Library.

ISBN 978 1 29227 992 3

Printed in the UK by Bell & Bain Ltd, Glasgow.

Acknowledgements

The author and publisher would like to thank the following individuals and organisations for permission to reproduce photographs:

123RF: ammentorp 43, blueskyimage 112, dgilder 75, kadmy 51, Jakkrit Orrasri 114, Andriy Popov 39, ronnarong thanuthattaphong 41, Undrey 129, Cathy Yeulet 29, HONGQI ZHANG 53; **Alamy:** Golden Pixels LLC 99, Ian Pilbeam 37; **Photolink/Photodisc:** F. Schussler 96; **Shutterstock:** Africa Studio 60, ALPA PROD 107, Shevel Artur 57, BasPhoto 15, Eliks 46, Leszek Glasner 87, Michaeljung 59, Monkey Business Images 121, Rawpixel.com 63, Henrik Winther Andersen 1.

Contents

About this book

This book is designed as a course companion, which will give you the tools you need to cover all the Knowledge, Skills and Behaviour requirements of the Apprenticeship standard as well as those set out in the Pearson amplification. The book covers all the modules within the Apprenticeship standard for Customer Service Practitioner Level 2 and helps prepare you for your end-point assessment (EPA). It will also help you identify and understand how to apply the appropriate skills and behaviours within your workplace. The handbook keeps you on track and focused on what you need to know to succeed, from the very start, through the Gateway, to a successful and rewarding apprenticeship.

Practical help in your role

Customer service practitioners are often the first point of contact for a customer; the first impression a customer has of a business or organisation. As a customer service practitioner your role is vital to customer satisfaction and their overall experience. You will need a vast amount of product and service knowledge as well as excellent people skills. In your apprenticeship, you will develop key behaviours, skills and knowledge that will allow you to fulfil this varied and exciting role.

This book will help you in your studies, and through your learning journey as an apprentice, but it is also supposed to help you in a practical way. The activities and scenarios are designed to be relatable and useful to your life and work so you can use them to learn and grow within your chosen job role. We hope you can use this book as a professional tool for your apprenticeship and beyond.

Features of the book

Features that enhance learning and understanding as well as prepare you for EPA such as:

- Knowledge, skills and behaviours linked together in an integrated fashion.
- Knowledge-based spreads that explain clearly and simply the content and concepts you need to understand.
- Skills-based spreads that provide opportunities for you to practise and develop the skills set out in the Standard.
- Dedicated EPA section which gives you practical advice, clear explanation of what to expect and helps you prepare for assessment as well as activities throughout to direct you to gather evidence for your portfolio and practise for EPA.
- Key term: concise definition of any technical terms you need to know.
- Scenario: helps to highlight behaviours you will need to identify or learn.
- Activity: contextualised to job roles and include questions.

- Professional working: embeds skills and behaviours in a professional context. Helps you to understand the 'how' and the 'why' of demonstrating the correct skills and behaviours in the context of your job.

- Link: directs you to other sections of the handbook that discuss the same topic.

Knowledge, Skills, Behaviours

The handbook integrates the three main aspects of the Apprenticeship assessment standards throughout. You will see the K icon for knowledge, S for skills and B for behaviour. See table below for which Knowledge, Skills and Behaviours are covered in each chapter:

Knowledge K	**Skills** S	**Behaviour** B
Understanding the organisation		*Equality*
Meeting regulations and legislation		*Equality*
Your role and responsibility		*Equality*
Systems and resources		
Product and service knowledge		
Knowing your customers		*Equality*
Customer experience	*Dealing with customer conflict and challenge*	*Equality*
	Communication	*Right first time*
	Interpersonal skills	*Being open to feedback* and *Teamworking*
	Influencing skills	
	Personal organisation	*Developing self* and *Presentation*

About the authors

Elizabeth Blaikie
Liz worked in education as an Assessor supporting learners in customer service and team leading, then progressed into quality assurance and management in the South East. She says the best part of the job is to see the confidence of learners grow as they move into managerial roles, progress to university and support new apprentices in their organisations. Liz has written assignments and support materials, it's her first venture into book writing, fulfilling another ambition.

Lambert Stewart
Lambert has been involved in training and customer service all of his working life in a wide variety of roles from retail to the Royal Family. He is a strong believer in the delivery of excellent customer service, and is currently in education as an Assessor and Tutor, working with colleges and private companies to support the development of their staff. He continually gains inspiration from seeing how well his students progress in their chosen field and go on to manage and encourage their teams to achieve the best.

Sue Tissiman
Sue works in the education sector supporting learners, providers and employers to develop their training provision and give learners and staff of all ages an opportunity to gain additional qualifications. Sue has contributed to quality assuring provision to ensure that there is outstanding focus on delivery and management of programmes. She says that one of the best aspects of her job is seeing the success of learners and their career progression.

1
Understanding the organisation

What is the purpose of an organisation?

Organisations provide goods and services to one or more of three business sectors: the private, public and voluntary sectors. Organisations are identified by their brand, which is their trademark. A brand sells 'the promise', or what the organisation promises the customer. In this module, you will learn about:

- the purpose of an organisation and brand promise
- an organisation's core values and how these link to service culture
- policies, procedures and legislation.

The purpose of an organisation and its brand promise

Organisations fall into one of three business sectors: private, public and voluntary. Regardless of which sector an organisation is in, its purpose is to provide a product or service that someone else wants. Its brand promise is the 'offer' or product it wants the consumer to purchase. Brands are often described by a short tagline (slogan) that is easy to remember and often accompanied by a logo.

Key terms

Profit – a financial benefit to a business that occurs when the amount of income generated is higher than the combined cost and expenses of running the business.

Taxes – compulsory sums of money paid by businesses to the government; a business pays different types of tax, such as value-added tax (VAT) or employment tax.

Suppliers – businesses work with external organisations who provide products or services at a cost to the business.

Shareholders – individuals or organisations who invest in a business by buying shares; shareholders are entitled to voting rights in appointing governors to a board of directors.

Brand – a type of product created by a particular organisation and usually unique to them in some way.

Mission statement – a written summary of an organisation's aims, goals and values.

Business sectors

Each business sector has a different purpose.

- The private sector exists to make a **profit** in order to pay **taxes** and the **suppliers**, staff and **shareholders** who invested in the business. Examples of private sector organisations could include computer companies and TV companies.
- The public sector needs to meet government targets and tends not to make a profit. Examples could include schools and colleges, and libraries.
- The voluntary sector raises money for good causes, without profit or the need to meet government targets. Examples could include charities and other non-governmental organisations (NGOs).

Activity

Advantages and disadvantages of business sectors

Research the three business sectors outlined above and complete the advantages and disadvantages columns in Table 1 to improve your understanding of each sector. Does each sector contribute financial benefits to the economy? Not every sector may appear to provide an obvious advantage or disadvantage but they do complement each other, helping to create a stronger economy.

Branding

All organisations are defined by a unique product or **brand**, which sets them apart from other businesses. The brand makes the organisation stand out and makes their product more attractive to the buyer, whether it is a phone, car or soft drink, for example. An organisation's **mission statement** defines the organisation as much as the brand. Check your organisation's mission statement and purpose.

Logos, registered trademarks or taglines define a product. Think of well-known sporting organisations and how their brands are defined. The brand promise becomes the unique selling point (USP). Advertisements promote new season stock, people buy new merchandise (goods) and profits go up. Advertising encourages fans to buy the new season kit and draws in people who want to support their sport, club or team. The kit promotes professionalism and competition in the team.

Sector	Aims or mission	Advantages	Disadvantages
Private	Organisations in the private sector may range from **sole traders** to multi-national organisations such as high-street chains with huge numbers of shareholders. They are often started by individuals with a passion for business – such as Jeff Bezos (owner of Amazon) or Bill Gates (founder of Microsoft) – with the aim of making large profits.		
Public	Public sector organisations include government-run institutions such as the NHS, and local council-run schools and libraries. These organisations are managed by a board of governors who support and advise on operations. Staff salaries are paid by the government and employees are called civil servants.		
Voluntary	Voluntary or not-for-profit organisations specialise in raising money to support those in need. They may operate abroad, providing housing or food supplies especially after natural disasters such as earthquakes, flooding or outbreaks of disease. Alternatively, they may operate at a local level, for example by helping homeless people or animal welfare shelters.		

Table 1: Advantages and disadvantages of the different business sectors

As a customer service practitioner, you can promote quality products or services to customers. Organisations want their core customers to visit regularly, spending money to increase profitability. To better understand sales and improve your productivity when selling, it helps to understand a brand's features and benefits. Good branding drives sales, customer retention and profits.

When selling to a customer, use emotive language to promote the product or service: in other words, create a dream. Well-known animated film companies create dreams. They then set up retail outlets to promote merchandise from the films, open theme parks, and this model is then copied internationally.

Activity

Think about your own organisation.

1. What sector does it fit into?
2. What is its mission statement and purpose?
3. What is its brand promise?
4. How do its aims relate to the sector you are in?

Key terms

Aim – something you want to achieve (an intention).

Sole trader – a business that is set up and controlled by one person; they take all the risk and profit relating to the business.

Summary

- By now you will know the sector in which your organisation operates and what the business produces.
- If you are not familiar with your organisation's mission statement, purpose or brand promise, research the main website to find out.
- Customers relate to a brand's purpose or promise; it will provide you with background information to help with customer service delivery.

Core values and how they link to service culture

Organisations are defined by their core values. Core values also help us to understand what is important to the organisation, and communicate the shared vision and brand, as well as how the organisation promotes its service culture.

Key terms

Social responsibility – the practice of producing goods and services that are not harmful to society.

Sustainability – managing natural resources so they are maintained for future need.

Equality – maintaining fairness of opportunity with regard to jobs, pay and promotion.

Service culture – organisations with an effective service culture train and reward staff that put the customer first.

Core values

Some organisations' values are **social responsibility**, **sustainability** or **equality**. Organisations with these values take pride in sharing their beliefs with their staff and customers.

A business that values sustainability, for example, might be a fishmonger who only sells locally caught fish from fishermen who don't overfish stock and who use large fishing nets that don't damage reefs. An example of a business that values equality might be a sports club that provides guidance on fairness and equality for women playing at international level in cricket, football, hockey, tennis and rugby, in line with equality legislation.

Service culture

Core values are related to **service culture** and competitiveness. In customer service roles, important values include:

- listening
- putting the customer first
- being attentive
- going beyond a customer's expectations to provide the best customer service for them.

Organisations that promote these core values may use motivation and reward to encourage staff to adopt these behaviours.

Look at Figure 1 to see behaviours that are important to a service culture.

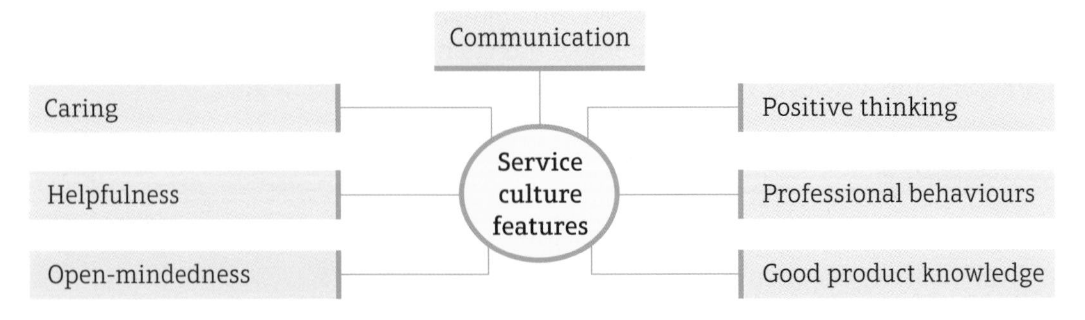

Figure 1: As a customer service practitioner these behaviours are important to you

An organisation with an effective service culture encourages its staff to communicate with customers and trains them in how to behave. It also regularly gathers customer feedback to check satisfaction levels, highlighting ways to improve delivery.
For example, a phone company may promote sustainability by asking customers to return old equipment for recycling. They need to make this easy for customers to do, by providing postage-paid return packaging for example. As a customer service practitioner, you should promote this service to customers.

As an employee, you could also demonstrate an organisation's core value of sustainability by reducing the number of pages you print, for example. Ask yourself whether printouts are really required: could they be emailed or viewed as a presentation?

Organisations may have dress codes or want customers to be greeted in a particular way. Staff should also have good product knowledge and the right attitude when helping customers. Staff behaviour may be rewarded with feedback such as 'great work' or recognition like 'staff member of the month'.

In the NHS, staff often work longer shifts to make sure patients have been cared for and that they are comfortable while waiting to see a doctor. If patients are in pain, they will provide pain relief where possible. In such cases, staff members are encouraged to see that their behaviours benefit the team and overall organisation.

Link 

Module 7: Customer experience

Training

Customer-friendly organisations will train new staff according to their code of practice, supporting them to meet the organisation's goals. Internal training from induction to specialist knowledge will motivate staff to learn new skills and behaviours. Organisations may introduce targets to motivate sales once basic training is established.

Not all organisations succeed in being customer focused: some do not fit the requirements of a service culture in terms of training and communication. Although they may have good products to offer, if staff are unprofessional or not correctly trained, problems will arise in service delivery.

Equality and diversity when dealing with customers

As an employee you have specific responsibilities for equality and diversity in your job role. These are linked to the Equality Act (2010), which you will learn about in the next module.

Link 

Module 2: Meeting regulations and legislation

Read your contract of employment and induction information to find statements on equality. Your responsibilities include treating everyone fairly. Equal opportunities legislation aims to prevent people being discriminated against. You can find more information about this on the Arbitration, Conciliation Advisory Service (ACAS) website.

In treating customers respectfully, you follow the organisation's equality policy, adapting your service approach to meet specific needs for all customers. Make sure you communicate in an open, fair and respectful manner with everyone. For example, it is unlawful for **service providers** to refuse to offer a service to someone with a disability or to offer disabled people a lower standard of service than anyone else.

Key term 

Service providers – individuals providing the service.

Values-based leadership and service culture

People are motivated by values. They care about their personal values and live their lives according to them. In other words, values make us enthusiastic. An organisation based around shared values is more flexible and productive than one in which management do not share the same aims and purpose.

Customer feedback

These days, customers are quick to promote their experiences on social media. People like sharing positive experiences with friends and family, and recommendations provide free marketing for an organisation. However, if people are unhappy with an experience, they can also be quick to complain.

On average, satisfied customers tell nine of their friends that they have had a good experience; an unhappy customer complains to 16 people! It is therefore vital to make sure customers have a good experience. Keeping existing customers satisfied means they will trust in your service.

Organisations can gather customer feedback to check satisfaction with a new purchase. You can capture informal feedback by chatting to customers on the shop floor, or conduct surveys via social media or email. Many organisations share customer testimonials and case studies on their websites to attract a wider audience. This shows they are listening to feedback, creating a good interaction with the customer.

Activity

Customer service on holiday

Scenario

Last year you went on a family holiday. There were a lot of problems: long queues at the airport; no hotel transfer coach; and you did not like the food at the hotel. You didn't enjoy the holiday! You didn't buy into the holiday company's promise of two weeks relaxing on the beach because their promise did not match your experience.

1. Think about your last holiday. Which of the following exceeded your customer service expectations?
   - The travel
   - The hotel
   - Eating out
   - Guided tours
2. What did you enjoy most about the overall holiday experience?
   - Professional service
   - Friendly staff
   - Location
   - Tourist sites
3. Have you attended an event in the last year?
   - Were you made to feel welcome on arrival?
   - Did the staff promote any merchandise?
   - Were you asked to promote the event on social media afterwards?
   - If so, did you offer feedback?

Activity

Find out the following information about your organisation

1. What evaluation tools does your organisation use to measure customer satisfaction?
2. Do they have staff meetings to discuss feedback?
3. Do they conduct staff surveys?
4. Does your organisation monitor how many complaints are made?
5. If a customer tells you that you handled a task really well, do you get written evidence of this?

Evaluation tools might include customer or staff satisfaction surveys or testimonials sent in by customers. Surveys provide data on what customers like or dislike, what service or stock they might like introduced for sale, and what is not working.

Core values and competitiveness

Organisations that we like to purchase from, such as high street brands offering a range of items from furniture to clothes, all share the same important customer service values (as shown in Figure 2). They share values with:

- a strong history of sustainability that appeals to all ages of shopper
- a simple concept as a brand
- a limit in the range of offers to customers.

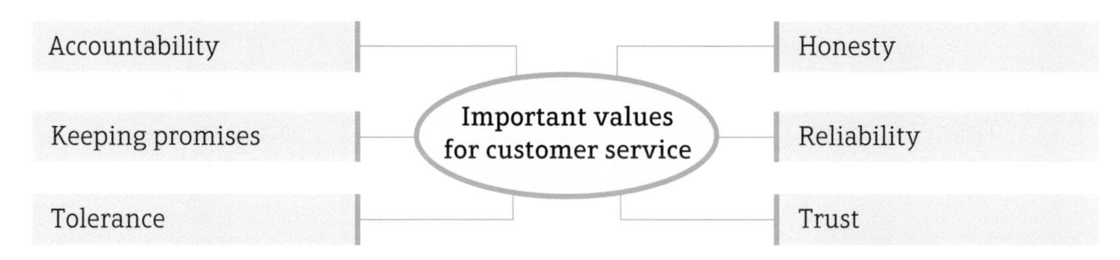

Figure 2: Important values for working in customer service

Service values are important to customer-focused organisations. They are likely to recruit staff that demonstrate the values shown in Figure 2. Staff with these values will also be more motivated to work at the organisation if they feel their values are respected by their employer. This forms a good employer–employee relationship. Do you feel valued at your place of work?

Activity

Your organisation

1. What are the core values of your organisation?
2. What is your organisation's brand promise?
3. What does the brand value tell customers about the organisation?
4. How are the values applied to customer service?

Summary

You should now:

- have an understanding of what your organisation's core values are and how they link to its service culture
- have researched your organisation's brand promise and be able to relate it to their mission statement
- understand that knowledge helps you engage with the team and gives you confidence in your job
- be able to work more productively and develop as a person.

Policies, procedures and legislation

All organisations will have in place policies and procedures that determine how they do business. They will also need to observe relevant legislation.

Key term 

Complaint – when a customer contacts an organisation to complain about its goods or services.

It is important to understand the difference between policies, procedures and legislation.

- Policies are statements that direct how an organisation conducts its services or business. An example might be a **complaints** policy, which provides guidance on what to do if a customer complains about a product or service.
- Procedures are a series of steps to be followed in order to achieve a specific outcome. An example might be how to communicate with a customer, or use a till point.
- Legislation is the process of providing laws or guidance. It defines what an organisation can and cannot do, providing legal guidance on a process or procedure. Organisations must abide by the law, or risk fines or damage to their reputations.

A policy may have accompanying procedures, such as the procedure for handling complaints that accompanies a complaints policy. Note that a policy can exist without a procedure, however, and vice versa.

Internal policies

Most organisations will have the examples of internal policies shown in Figure 3, which are set by board members.

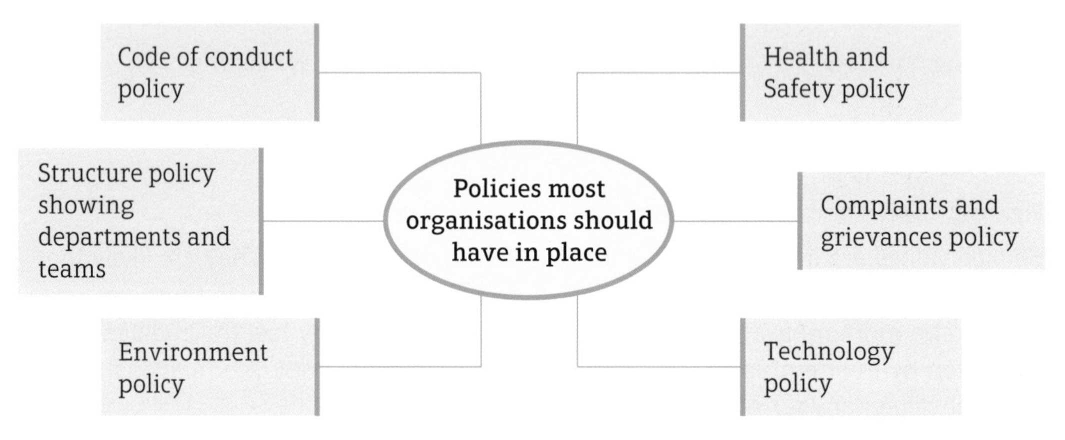

Figure 3: There are a number of policies that most organisations should have in place

Health and Safety

This policy provides guidance for employees, from the level of individual responsibility and knowing who to report to in your department, to what to do in an emergency (such as a fire evacuation). Ask about the Health and Safety policy at your organisation. Find out who the organisation is insured with (on the Employer Liability Insurance).

Health and Safety legislation has been developed to protect individuals in the workplace and to minimise their risk of injury. Organisations should have clear guidance on the responsibilities they have to the health, safety and welfare of visitors and employees.

Technology

This policy should take into account any changes in legislation regarding technology. Staff must be properly trained in how to use equipment. Failure to train staff might result in financial penalties for the business. Policies must cover the use of laptops, phones or mobile devices; these devices must be encrypted to protect personal and business information.

Legislation developed under the Data Protection Act (2018) ensures that business and personal information is stored safely and securely. Information must not be shared with anyone who does not have the right to access that information. The General Data Protection Regulations (GDPR) were developed to give people greater control over how their personal data is stored. Organisations can be fined for misuse of data storage and for passing on data to third parties.

Human resources (HR)

This policy relates to staff: personal information, recruitment, induction, training and development, annual leave and absence, grievance and complaints issues, and the management of policies. Often HR is outsourced to external organisations to reduce **overheads**. HR information must be stored in a locked cabinet and access to it should be limited. Electronic files may not be accessible to certain staff and files may need to be encrypted if they are used on a laptop.

Most organisations will check references, education and qualifications of new staff and conduct a thorough check on their background and employment history. Depending on your organisation, external government services may carry out an enhanced check such as a Disclosure and Barring Service (DBS). They may ask you to complete a personality questionnaire or to attend an assessment centre for in-depth checks. They want to ensure that you fit with the organisation and the job offered.

Legislation relating to HR departments covers data protection, confidentiality, equal opportunities, discrimination, employment law, the minimum wage and financial regulations. HR must ensure that staff follow policies and procedures and adhere to legislation at all times, for example by following the grievance procedure for complaints.

Key terms 

Copyright – protects the creator of a piece of work (which could be creative work or work produced during work time).

Hierarchy chart (organogram) – shows the reporting lines in a team, department or organisation and how the job roles relate to each other.

Overheads – the running costs of a business (taxes, lighting, heating, etc.).

Confidentiality

No business wants to lose sensitive information: this would break data protection laws, resulting in financial penalties and loss of trust. The exact details of this policy will depend on your organisation. Government or professional organisations might ask you to sign a confidentiality clause preventing you from discussing business information with other people within a given timeframe. The policy might cover international and national **copyright**, the ability to work for a competitor organisation and restrictions on sharing client information for three years. It should also cover computer security, passwords and screen locking.

Structure of the business

As a business expands, HR often produce a **hierarchy chart (organogram)** showing the departments in the organisation and the manager for each department. This helps employees to see reporting lines. Department charts show the individuals in each team, with their job titles. Hierarchy charts show how individuals and teams are interlinked.

Key term 

ACAS – The Advisory, Conciliation and Arbitration Service is a government body that provides advice to employers and employees on all aspects of employment rights.

Complaints or grievances

This policy governs grievances and complaints. A procedure sets out the reporting process and details who manages the complaint, the given timeframe to resolve the issue and, if it cannot be resolved, how it should be escalated (taken to a higher level) to a tribunal or **ACAS**. ACAS resolve difficult issues with specialist staff who act as a third party to provide alternative resolutions.

If a customer complains about a product or service:

- take notes and report the complaint to a supervisor
- discuss the complaint afterwards to understand how to deal with it
- research the organisation's grievance policy to improve your understanding of the complaints process.

Consider how to deal with confrontation and complaints from customers. If a customer is angry, listen, take notes and, if you are not sure what action to take, find a supervisor and ask for advice. Your organisation will have a complaints policy providing guidance on what to do if someone complains.

The complaints process usually follows the three steps shown in Table 2.

Complaint	Action
Complaint of faulty goods made to member of staff	Member of staff not sure what to do so passes to line manager
Complaint assessed by line manager	Line manager discusses with customer
Line manager follows procedure	Offers refund, voucher or replacement goods or services

Table 2: The complaints process

A complaint might come from a colleague (an internal customer) if they are unhappy with something you have done. In this case, discuss the issue with a supervisor and arrange to chat with the person who made the complaint. See how you can resolve the problem and listen carefully to any advice provided. Complaints policies usually state that the complaint must be dealt with in a given timeframe (usually 10 days). However, if it is a straightforward refund or replacement, then it can be dealt with straightaway. Follow your organisation's procedures at all times, but be aware of the legislation affecting complaints.

Activity

Policies and procedures in your workplace

1. Find and read the policies and procedures relevant to your job role in customer service.
2. Find and read the complaints procedure.
3. Find out how to report an issue or complaint.
4. Is there a dress code for staff?
5. Are you expected to wear a specific colour to work?
6. Is your work-wear appropriate in a customer-facing role?

Activity

Gaining feedback

Ask two separate colleagues for their feedback on how you dealt with two customer-facing situations: one in which you performed well and one that could have been improved.

Professional working

The two examples below outline best practice when following procedures and policies in a customer service environment. Example 1 shows how you could handle a customer who was annoyed with something you said. Example 2 shows how you could handle a customer who complained about a product or service.

Example 1 – an annoyed customer

Follow procedure and listen to the customer, who may have misunderstood something you said. It may help to repeat the information in a way they will understand. Make sure your body language and tone of voice is friendly. Most customers find it hard to stay annoyed with someone who is trying to help them, especially if that person smiles. Make sure you give consistent professional customer service to customers so they get quality service at all times.

Example 2 – a customer complaint

Follow procedure and listen to the customer voice their complaint, then explain that complaints need to be handled by a line manager. Explain to the customer that you will get a line manager to listen to their complaint and take action accordingly. Listen to how the complaint is dealt with by your line manager and learn from the experience.

Activity

Making complaints

1. What action should you take if you get a complaint?
2. Who should you report to?
3. Does the complaint need to be written down?
4. Should you apologise to the customer?

Summary

- Now that you have examined the policies and procedures at your organisation, you should be familiar with the guidelines that apply to your work role.
- Professional working practice helps to drive up standards in organisations.
- Try to keep up with any changes so that you are able to deliver excellent customer service practice.

Digital media policies

Organisations must ensure they have an up-to-date digital media policy that explains how personal information is used in a social media setting, to cover issues relating to copyright, confidentiality and privacy.

Link

Module 2: Meeting regulations and legislation

Digital guidelines

Digital guidelines were updated in the Data Protection Act (2018) to make them fit for purpose in the digital age. This updated UK law includes General Data Protection Regulations (GDPR), which make it unacceptable for data breaches to occur. As part of these changes, anyone can ask to stop receiving marketing information or unsubscribe from websites at any time.

Digital media is content that can be communicated over the internet or by computer. It covers:

- text (emails)
- audio and video content
- graphics (pictures and logos)
- information from a newspaper or network such as a blog or website.

The purpose of digital guidelines is to ensure that staff keep business and personal information secure. If necessary, files should be encrypted when transferring data from one site to another.

Digital legislation has been updated to keep up with developments in digital technology. Most organisations will have a digital policy to monitor the use of social and digital media at work. This will cover the use of mobile phones, cyber-bullying, the use of photographs, the protection of personal data and exploitation.

Policies in customer service organisations should cover digital media and the GDPR, along with other policies, guidelines and regulations relevant to the business.

Social media

Guidelines in a social media policy should link to the organisation's mission statement. Employees should be trained in how to use social media to ensure that they act professionally, ethically and in a clear (transparent) way that is integrated into the organisation.

The aims and **objectives** for a digital policy should:

- cover communication: how to use social media to promote products and distribute information to customers and employees
- provide creative interest in the organisation by showcasing work, careers and cultural values
- embed digital technology, putting the customer first.

As part of your organisation's digital media policy, and with the guidance of your line manager, you should manage and monitor data input and output, use data tracking, set targets and budget responsibilities, and agree creative content for the organisation.

The acceptable use of social media during work time should be set out in a code of conduct. If someone tags their workplace on their profile, for example, their settings are not private and they are representing the organisation to the general public.

Language (and conversations) should be professional and should not show the organisation in a bad light.

Key term

Objective – something that is aimed for; a goal.

Professional working

Customer service practitioners must remember that business information is confidential and should not be shared on social media. Photos of colleagues should not be posted without a privacy setting as this would breach confidentiality and is illegal. People should always be asked for permission to use their photo.

Employees should have training on social media. A supervisor should approve official messages before they are posted, deal with security concerns and create content that represents the organisation professionally.

There are legal risks if you use someone else's content and post it without approval. You are also not allowed to make money by posting business information. This is illegal and against confidentiality and copyright agreements. To reduce risks, organisations should ensure that emails, spam and malware are monitored and checked regularly, with a sufficient firewall in place to protect the business. Copyright permission must be provided before reproducing, distributing or performing protected, or similar, work. Always check if you have permission to copy and use information at work.

Social media includes:

- social networking sites
- video/photo/audio-sharing sites
- online platforms
- instant messaging
- blogs
- email and text messaging
- presentations
- podcasts.

Summary

Check your use of digital media at work. Think before using it next time. To reinforce how to use social media applications, organise an event for yourself at home using social media. Try to use methods that were discussed in this module: be creative and colourful!

The following activities will help you to strengthen the skills you have learned in this module about understanding the organisation.

Activities

Personal development

- Do you think data protection laws offer sufficient protection for electronic data?
- Has your organisation provided training on working safely and securely?
- Does your organisation provide training on new legislation?
- Did you find your organisation's complaints procedure?

EPA preparation

Summarise the evidence you have gathered into a report or slide presentation explaining the following topics:

- the sector your organisation operates in, including the purpose
- your organisation's core values and service culture, and how they relate to each other
- the products and services offered by your organisation
- your organisation's brand promise – what does it tell customers about the organisation?
- three regulations or pieces of legislation relating to customer service that affect how you deliver customer service at work
- the impact of non-compliance
- how the ethical standards and code of practice effect the ways in which your organisation delivers customer service
- the evaluation tools used to measure service delivery.

Save the evidence in your apprentice showcase.

Reflective account

Review your understanding of how your organisation operates. Take time to reflect and make notes: the information will sink in the more you use it.

2

Meeting regulations and legislation

How does legislation affect you and your organisation?

As a customer service practitioner it is important that you understand regulations and legislation. Your organisation will have guidelines on this. In this module, you will learn how these rules may affect your customers: their consumer rights, their right to privacy and data protection. You should also be aware of legislation that affects your own employment and your safety at work. In your role, it will also be important that you ensure that both customers and employees are treated equally. In this module you will learn:

- which pieces of legislation and regulations affect you and your organisation
- what your responsibilities are regarding legislation and how to apply them when delivering customer service.

Know the legislation and regulations that affect your organisation

You need to be familiar with relevant legislation and regulations in order to understand how they affect you and your organisation, and your role as a customer service practitioner. Consumer protection legislation, for example, provides clear and accurate guidance to customers on their rights, and organisations must provide relevant policies and procedures to meet these requirements.

Legislation you need to know

Table 1 sets out important legislation for the customer service industry.

Legislation	Purpose
Consumer Rights Act (2015)	This replaces three major pieces of consumer legislation: the Sale of Goods Act, Unfair Terms in Consumer Contracts Regulations, and the Supply of Goods and Services Act. All goods must be of **satisfactory quality**, fit for purpose and as described by the organisation. This includes digital content.
Consumer Credit Act (1974)	This regulates credit card purchases and also provides protection when entering into a **loan or hire agreement**. It gives you the right to a cooling-off period of five days and a further 14-day cooling-off period during which time you can change your mind.
Trade Descriptions Act (1968)	It is an offence for a trader to make misleading or incorrect statements about goods and services. **Trading standards officers** enforce the legislation; they fine traders if, for example, traders describe goods incorrectly or make false statements about accommodation or services.
Consumer Protection Act (1987)	This protects the public by stopping the manufacture and supply of unsafe goods. It makes the manufacturer or seller responsible for a defective product and for any damage caused. It allows councils to suspend the sale of unsafe goods and to seize them. It also prevents misleading pricing.
Consumer Contracts Regulations (2013)	These provide rights for shopping online and offer protection if something goes wrong. The regulations also cover sales made over the phone. The trader must provide a description of the goods, the total price, payment, delivery charges, costs for returning goods, right to cancel, information on the seller and information on digital compatibility with hardware or software.
Equality Act (2010)	There are nine characteristics of the Equality Act: age, disability, gender reassignment, marriage or civil partnership, pregnancy or maternity, race, religion, sex and sexual orientation. The Act also protects against discrimination by association (for example, if you are discriminated against because your child is gay).

Key terms

Satisfactory quality – products or services must be of a 'satisfactory' standard for the consumer to want to purchase them.

Loan or hire agreement – an agreement between two parties who decide on terms and conditions for the purchase of goods or services.

Trading standards officer – people who advise consumers and businesses about legislation relating to the buying, selling and hiring of goods and services.

Data Protection Act (1998) and Data Protection Act (2018), including General Data Protection Regulations (GDPR)	You have a right to know what personal data organisations hold about you and can request access to view that information. You can ask an organisation not to hold or use information that causes damage or distress, and you can request that they withhold information (for example, if you are being investigated for a crime). Under the GDPR you can choose not to share your information for marketing purposes. You can also unsubscribe from marketing emails and request that companies stop using your data for direct marketing promotions.
Health and Safety at Work Act (1974)	This ensures a safe place of work, a safe system of work, safe **equipment, machinery and plant**, and safe and competent people around you. Employers must carry out risk assessments and take steps to eliminate or control those risks. They must tell workers about hazards, and provide training and supervision.

Table 1: Legislation you need to know when working in customer service

Key term 

Equipment, machinery and plant – this refers to the land, buildings, office equipment, vehicles (cars, trucks, forklift machinery), furniture and so on used by organisations to carry out their day-to-day business.

Consumer-related legislation

Consumer protection prevents poor business practice, stops fraud and protects consumers from unfair selling practices. Consumer legislation provides guidance to traders and consumers, protecting the general public. Information on goods and services must be clear, accurate and must not mislead consumers.

Consumer protection prevents:

- pyramid selling – this is when someone operates a scheme in which a consumer pays to receive a greater reward by introducing other consumers to the scheme
- false selling – this is when an organisation claims that goods or products have been approved for use when they have not
- aggressive sales – this is when a customer is strongly advised not to leave the premises until a contract has been signed, or when a sales representative refuses to leave the home of a consumer before a contract has been signed
- someone demanding that goods you received are returned at your own expense when you did not order them in the first place.

Non-compliance with consumer-related legislation and regulations can lead to:

- financial penalties (organisations may have to pay a fine)
- loss of trust from consumers
- prosecution
- customer dissatisfaction
- damage to the brand.

Activity

Legislation Acts

Look back at Table 1 and give examples of how each Act effects your role. You can also research the different pieces of legislation on the internet. For each Act, state what the implications are of non-compliance (i.e. what would happen if you or your organisation did not follow the law?).

Key term 

Non-compliance – failing to comply with (act on) a rule, regulation or law.

Summary 

- Legislation and regulatory requirements can be challenging to remember, but you need to be aware of them for your job and also for your own consumer protection.
- Consumer protection provides guidance for customer service practitioners: be aware of the regulations and legal aspects at work and home.

Equality

As a customer service practitioner you must comply with equality legislation. This is outlined in the Equality Act (2010) which has nine protected characteristics (see Figure 1).

Equality in your job role

In your department at work, you may find a range of professional people who are more or less experienced than you. Treat everyone with respect and learn from everyone. Your colleagues will be happy to share their knowledge and experience if you behave appropriately and respectfully. You may have a situation that worries you: ask them questions about how they would deal with a similar situation and listen attentively to their answers.

Working in a diverse organisation means that there is a range of people from different cultures and backgrounds. Individuals bring new ideas and ways of working to an organisation, making it a more creative and pleasant working environment. You may hear different languages at work, see people observing different religious holidays and work with a wide range of age groups. Diversity broadens our knowledge of language, makes us more creative, encourages us to listen to experiences from other people and makes us more open-minded.

Equality means treating everyone fairly and with respect. Treat your colleagues with respect and professionalism. As an employee you have specific responsibilities for equality and diversity as you perform your role within the workplace. This means that you should treat everyone fairly regardless of age, disability, gender reassignment, marriage and civil partnership, pregnancy and maternity, race, religion or belief, sex or sexual orientation (as shown in Figure 1).

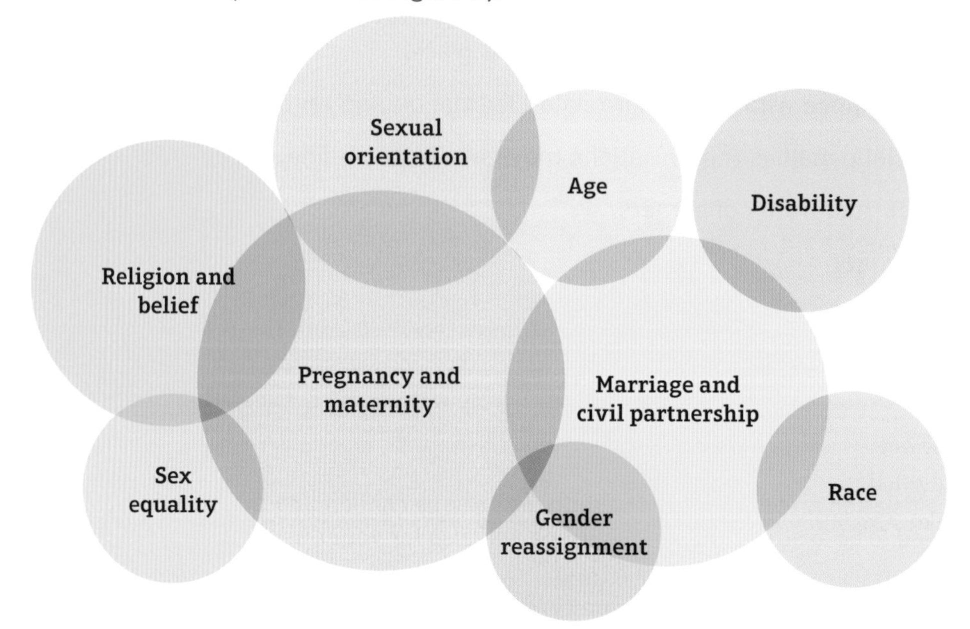

Figure 1: The nine protected characteristics of equality and diversity

Follow your organisation's equality policy. Communicate in a respectful way so that customers understand you, ensuring that you meet their specific needs. You may not recognise if a customer has a disability or needs help, especially if you are talking with them over the phone or communicating by email. Remember to treat everyone fairly and equally. If a customer is in a wheelchair, it is easier to recognise the disability. How would you know if a customer was partially sighted or a little hard of hearing, however?

Scenario

Callum went to the library with his sister. They had recently moved into the area and wanted some books for the holidays. They approached the customer service desk. It was a quiet period and the librarian welcomed them to the library. They had proof of identity (passports) but had forgotten a reference letter for Callum as he was under 18, and a proof of address for his sister. Callum was partially sighted and had a hearing problem due to a skateboarding accident. His sister asked if there was a hearing loop and audio books available for Callum.

They completed their application forms and said they would return with the right proof of their address. The librarian explained about **e-books**, screen-reading technology and helplines such as **AbilityNet** where they could get help using a computer and the internet.

Callum thought it would be easier to download a selection of e-books onto his **e-reader** as it could enlarge the print and change the background to make it easier to read. The librarian was helpful and his sister intended to go back.

Key terms

e-books – books that are in an electronic rather than paper format so they can be downloaded onto a computer.

AbilityNet – free helpline providing advice and information for disabled people on the use of computers and the internet.

e-reader – a hand-held reading device that allows multiple books and films to be downloaded for viewing.

Activity

Providing customer service to partially sighted people

Partially sighted people can be highly independent but, as a customer service practitioner, it is always helpful to offer information to individuals in case they need it. For example, research the following:

- Where can you find the best information for partially sighted people? You could start by looking at the websites for the Royal Society for the Blind and the Royal National Institute of Blind People (RNIB). Do they offer free advice on home and work life?
- Are e-books free to download?
- Are video magnifiers available for computer use?

Non-compliance with equality legislation may result in financial penalties, so treat all customers with respect, fairness and professionalism.

Summary

- Customers come from many different backgrounds and will have many different individual requirements. They may also be unfamiliar with the products or services provided by your organisation.
- Make sure you have information to hand so that people can make their own decisions based on the information you give them.
- Remember that non-compliance with equality legislation means you are discriminating against customers. If you do not comply with legislation, it will affect the reputation of the organisation and cause loss of trust in the brand.

Know your responsibility in relation to legislation and how to apply it when delivering customer service

Key term

Contract of employment – this forms the agreement between employer (your organisation) and employee (you). It helps you understand what employers expect of you during your employment with them. It outlines the terms and conditions that you agree to, for example hours of work, location, duties, time off, sick pay, holidays, confidentiality agreement, IT policy and termination of contract conditions.

Your responsibilities at work should be outlined for you in your job description or your **contract of employment**. Your employer will show you the policies, procedures and regulations that you must follow in the workplace, including those relating to legislation. These will show you how your organisation expects you to communicate with customers, and how to behave and treat individuals with respect and fairness.

Professional working

A contract of employment provides guidance on your responsibilities to your employer. It confirms your expectations of the job and demonstrates your trust in your employer when you sign. Your employer is not obliged to give you a written contract. The contract is, however, a useful document to have as it shows you the terms agreed with your employer. Most employers issue a written contract because, without one, you would only need to give your employer one week's notice if you wanted to leave their employment. This would give your employer very little time to replace you.

Further guidance on your responsibilities will be provided in your organisation's policies and procedures, including information about data protection and confidentiality. It is not acceptable to say you are not aware of them so take time to find out what they are. If you break the rules you will face a disciplinary meeting and may be dismissed.

Why is it important to keep information confidential within an organisation?

The data your employer holds about you and your customers is protected by the Data Protection Act (1998), which outlines the specific ways in which data can be used. It is your responsibility and the responsibility of your employer to ensure that the data is stored safely and securely so that it cannot be accessed by people outside of the organisation. In order to help protect people in an increasingly digital world, the Data Protection Act (1998) was replaced by the Data Protection Act (2018), which includes the General Data Protection Regulations (GDPR).

The Data Protection Act (1998) was similar to the GDPR but it did not have the powers that have been introduced relating to transparency for individuals. Table 2 lists the main principles of the 1998 Act and details the impact that they had.

The Data Protection Act (1998) – eight main principles	Impact
Fairly and lawfully processed	There must be valid grounds for using and collecting personal data; consideration must be given to how data is handled and individuals must not be deceived or misled when personal data is collected
Processed for limited purposes	The purpose of recording documentation must be clear and explained to individuals from the start; if personal data is to be stored for a new purpose, organisations must check that it is compatible with the original purpose and consent is provided
Data must be adequate, not excessive	Organisations must not store large amounts of data on individuals
Accurate and up to date	Organisations should agree how long information can be stored before it is deleted or closed, for example, if a member of staff stops working there, the staff file could be deleted after three years
Stored for no longer than necessary	Organisations should have a policy detailing the duration of data storage on individuals
Technical and organisational steps taken against unauthorised or unlawful processing of personal data, loss or damage to data	Security measures should be appropriate to ensure the data stored is protected, for example firewalls, encryption, etc.
Data must be processed in accordance with the rights of data subjects under legislation	Permission must be given for data to be collected by the individual either verbally or in writing; personal data should be adequate, relevant and up to date
Personal data must not be transferred outside of the EU unless adequate provision of protection is provided for the data	Data must not be sold on to third parties who act unscrupulously (being dishonest or unfair) and sell information overseas

Table 2: The eight main principles of the Data Protection Act (1998)

Activity

Legislation

Consider whether you think the legislation (as shown in Table 1 on pages 16–17) has gone far enough. Do you think it could have done more?

Be considerate and respect other people. You would not want your own personal or business information discussed by the team.

As an employee, you cannot 'share' information with people around you. Part of the employee–employer relationship is keeping information safe and confidential. Report your concerns if you think your computer has been hacked or if you email the wrong person with business information.

Professional working

Check your understanding of working practices.

1. Do you:
   - close the computer screen when leaving your desk?
   - change your password regularly?
   - log off at the end of your shift?
2. If you work on a confidential report, do you:
   - change the screen if someone stands behind you?
   - lock the report away when leaving your desk?
   - only share it with the person who requested it?
3. If you deal with a complaint, do you:
   - refer to the individual?
   - discuss the issue with the office?
   - discuss the complaint with your line manager?

Scenario

Connie Diva writes the music and lyrics for the band *Fainthearted*. She is also their lead singer. She earns royalties when the songs are played on the radio. She tours with three musicians who want a bigger share of the profits. The band is paid a flat rate, which is standard in the music business. Connie writes her songs while on tour. They are about personal events in her life. Connie copyrights her lyrics and music before sharing them, to protect them and to ensure that she keeps the royalties. The band complain to the manager that they are not earning enough and, at the end of the tour, Connie lets them go. She gets a new band for the next tour.

If you design something at work, it belongs to the organisation. Connie Diva wrote her music and lyrics in her own time, and she copyrighted her work to protect it.

What information needs to be kept confidential within your organisation?

Information that needs to be kept confidential relates to:

- customers' personal and financial data
- employees' personal and financial information
- business data.

Under data protection legislation, everyone has the right for their data to be stored correctly and securely.

Business and personal information belongs to the organisation and remains confidential. It is your responsibility to keep information safe and confidential.

What are the implications of letting someone else use the computer when you are logged on?

Allowing someone to use your computer when you are logged on is a breach of security. You should not share information with other people as it is confidential. If the other person entered incorrect financial information, for example, you could face disciplinary action and potentially lose your job as it is against data protection, GDPR and confidentiality legislation.

Activity

Your understanding on sharing information

1. If you design a poster for your department:
   - do you own it?
   - does the organisation own it?
   - can you take it home?
2. If you develop something that will help customer service delivery:
   - do you benefit?
   - do customers benefit?
   - does the organisation benefit?
3. If you design something at work, do you discuss it with:
   - your line manager?
   - your colleagues and friends?
   - your family?

Data Protection Act

1. How does the Data Protection Act (1998) and (2018), including GDPR, affect you at work?
2. What are the implications of non-compliance with data protection and the GDPR?
3. What would happen if you or your organisation did not follow the law?

Security and targets

1. Why is security important at work? Suggest three areas of work where security is particularly important.
2. Daily targets are part of everyday work. What might be the impact of not meeting your targets? Give three examples.

Summary

- When you start working, it can be difficult to remember the different policies, regulations and legislation you need for your job.
- Think about the scenarios in this sub-topic and apply them at work. If you apply them outside of work, in different situations, it will eventually become second nature.

Health and safety

You have a responsibility to take care of your own health and safety as well as the health and safety of other people affected by your actions at work.

What are your responsibilities under the Health and Safety at Work Act (1974)?

You have a responsibility to manage stress levels by keeping fit, healthy and hydrated, especially if you work in a competitive office and regularly chase deadlines and targets. If a team is not productive, they will impact the department objectives and customer service delivery will be affected. This may result in:

- absenteeism (time off work)
- low morale (a lack of enthusiasm and confidence)
- poor customer service
- mistakes
- reduced confidence in the business
- legal consequences
- loss of loyalty
- reduced strength of competition.

Stress and wellbeing are recognised states of mind in the workplace. If an employee is stressed they do not function as well as someone who is customer focused. Discuss mental health issues with your line manager and seek support if you feel you need it.

What are your employer's responsibilities under the Health and Safety at Work Act (1974)?

Your employer has a duty of care to keep you, other employees and customers safe in the workplace. When you started working at your organisation you may have had induction training, including a tour of the building, health and safety training, information on technology and IT, and guidance on where to find policies and procedures. To find out what you remember about this induction training, complete the following activity.

Activity

Staying safe in the workplace

Make a plan of your organisation, showing where fire extinguishers and emergency exits are located. Add the meeting point in case of evacuation, the name of a first aider and a fire warden, details of where the first-aid box is stored and the location of an accident reporting book, as detailed in Figure 2.

Make sure your plan looks professional in case you want to show it to your line manager. You can add any special responsibilities, such as health and safety training. Add the map to your apprentice showcase.

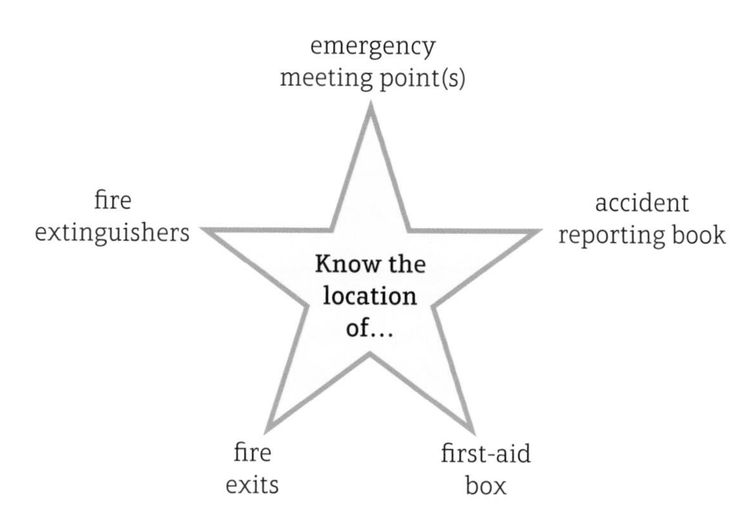

Figure 2: To stay safe at work, do you know where these things are?

Other aspects of health and safety include:

1. Personal protective equipment (PPE): depending on the working environment, employers must provide specialised equipment to protect against health risks. For example, on a construction site employees must complete site safety tests before going on site, and they must wear protective boots, high visibility vests and a hard hat at all times. As a customer service practitioner you may not need to use any PPE, but you may need to know how to use eye goggles, depending on where you work.
2. Manual handling: employers must provide manual handling training if employees need to move heavy boxes.
3. Display-screen equipment: take breaks from computers and video screens regularly to reduce repetitive strain injury and eye problems.

Activity

How regulations apply to your role

Check which regulations apply to your job role. Discuss the legislation and regulations with your line manager to ensure you understand how it affects you. There may be specialist regulations in your industry that have not been covered in this module.

Summary

- Understand what is expected of you as an employee in case of an evacuation or emergency situation. Your employer has a duty of care to employees and visitors to the organisation.
- Keep safe at work and when you are visiting other organisations.
- Take responsibility for making sure that you work safely and look after those people around you.

Codes of practice and ethical standards

Key terms

Codes of practice – written guidelines on how you should behave in your organisation.

Professional body – a not-for-profit group that oversees and regulates a particular profession, providing advice and support.

Ethical standards – principles that promote trust and fair behaviour.

Codes of practice are used across all industries and are usually created by a **professional body** of people who oversee a particular industry, and who advise professionals on standards of behaviour. The codes give advice on things like how to resolve customer confrontation and complaints.

Codes of practice can cover everything from an organisation's 'mission statement' (a statement that describes the organisation's key aims) to specific terms and conditions of employment. These elements may be contained in an induction pack or held in a key area of the organisation's website or internal network.

Codes of practice also include guidance on:

- dress code
- the use of personal or business mobile phones and electronic equipment
- business travel/expenses
- professional conduct.

Organisations might offer equal treatment on benefits, maternity and paternity leave, time off for bereavement (loss of a loved one), tuition or learning activities, and jury duty. Separate rules cover smoking, discipline and harassment.

Ethical standards promote human values such as fairness, trust and professional behaviours. They also provide guidelines about unethical behaviours, such as dishonesty or discrimination. They are different to codes of practice, which establish expected behaviours based on legal rather than ethical standards.

The consequences of not following codes of practice and ethical standards

If an organisation fails to follow codes of practice and ethical standards they might face financial penalties, loss of confidence in their product and the loss of jobs. Legislation and regulations relate to you as a customer service practitioner and to the consumer. Look at your organisation's policy on complaints and dealing with customer problems.

Codes of practice also cover how to deal with customer complaints, such as refunds and the replacement of goods or services. Ask your line manager how to deal with difficult situations. Until you have training or have observed several complaints, try not to deal with them on your own. Customers may want to deal with someone experienced if there is a problem. If a customer approaches you and asks for help, listen and take notes, but explain that you are not sure how to deal with the situation and get support. Customer complaints might include damaged goods or missed deliveries.

Activity

Customer complaints

Can you think of other complaints that customers might make? Have you dealt with any other types of complaints?

Non-compliance with regulations

Non-compliance under the Health and Safety at Work Act (1974) is a criminal offence and you could face prosecution by the **Health and Safety Executive (HSE)**. Consequences range from financial penalties to imprisonment. If an employee is injured at work they can **sue** the employer for not providing a safe place of work. It is important the employer provides you with basic training in health and safety.

Codes of practice relevant to you as a customer service practitioner

As an employee you have rights and responsibilities to protect yourself. Your employer should also make sure the workplace is a mutually respectful and safe environment. You should, as part of your induction, have been informed about the opportunities available within your organisation so that you know how to progress to the next level.

You can find more information and advice on your industry and occupation through your trade union. General information is available on the internet through the National Careers Service and **job boards** such as Monster and Total Jobs.

There is a range of representative bodies across all industries that listen to and represent the views of a group of people with common interests.

You should know:

- if there are any trade unions relevant to your occupation, representing and protecting the common interests of employees
- if there are any professional bodies relevant to your industry and occupation
- if there are any regulatory bodies relevant to your industry and occupation
- the name and role of the standards-setting organisation relevant to your occupation.

Activity

Employer responsibilities in the workplace

Think about your employer's responsibilities at work and why they should have these responsibilities.

Codes of practice

Which codes of practice affect you in your job role?

Ethical considerations and customer service

Organisations develop their own standards for employees to follow and set out the ways in which they expect them to behave.

Customers also make ethical decisions on a daily basis. You may have seen in the news the impact on companies who have been exposed for not paying tax.

An organisation can demonstrate these ethical considerations in a variety of ways, through advertising, posters or point-of-sale displays.

Key terms

Health and Safety Executive (HSE) – a group that is responsible for managing health, safety and risk management in the workplace. It provides guidance, posters, templates and literature relating to health and safety for employees and employers.

Sue: to take legal action against an individual or organisation.

Job boards – online recruitment sites providing details of available jobs.

Summary

- Codes of practice and ethical standards affect all organisations and everyone has to follow them. They are there to make sure we comply with behaviours such as equality and professional working.
- Make sure you know which regulations apply to your job role and how they affect you. If you are unsure, discuss this with your line manager. (There may be specialist regulations in your industry that have not been covered in this module.)

The following activities will help you to strengthen the skills you have learned in this module about meeting regulations and legislation.

Activities

Reflective account

You have now reviewed relevant legislation, regulations, codes of conduct and ethical standards. How did it go? Reflect on the various policies to help you remember them and list them in your apprentice showcase. The more you understand about the legislation, regulatory requirements, codes of practice and ethical standards in your workplace, the more confidence you will have in difficult situations. This knowledge and awareness will also help you approach situations both in and out of work.

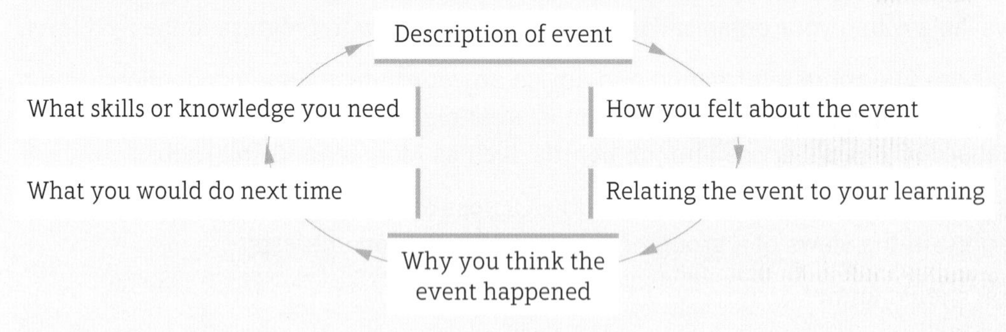

Figure 3: You can use the reflective cycle to help you reflect on your work

EPA preparation

Bring together all the activities you have completed throughout this module to improve your understanding of relevant regulations and legislation. The work you have done can be used as evidence for your end-point assessment presentation. Make sure that it looks professional and presentable.

Behaviours

Provide an example of each of the following:

1. an ethical standard that affects you at work
2. legislation that affects you at work
3. a code of conduct that affects you at work.

Although learning about legislation, regulations and codes of practice can be challenging, it will help you as both an employee and a consumer. The next time you need to complain about an issue at work you will be more aware of your rights and how you should approach the situation. If you need to return faulty goods to a store, you will be more aware of their customer service and of your rights as a consumer.

3

Your role and responsibility

What are your responsibilities?

Now that you have started your new job, you need to understand exactly what your job title means, the responsibilities that are outlined in your job description, your job targets and your role in the team.

Some organisations refer to targets as key performance indicators (KPIs): these link to both team and organisation targets. In developing the skills and knowledge required to manage your targets you will become an effective team member and deliver excellent customer service. You will do this by:

- understanding your role and responsibility (within your organisation), and the impact of your actions on others
- knowing the targets you must deliver against.

Understand your role and responsibility within your organisation

Key terms

Line manager – the person you report to at work.

Buddy – someone who supports you at work and provides advice.

Colleague – someone in your team who works alongside you.

Service standards – these define what a customer can expect and provide guidance to employees about the level of work they are expected to produce.

You and your **line manager** will agree tasks for you to complete as part of your job description. Your line manager may assign a '**buddy**' (or another **colleague**) to support you. Ask them questions about where to find policies, **service standards** and information. Remember that your actions will affect the team.

Your job role and responsibility

A job title provides guidance on your role and responsibilities in the organisation. Specific duties will be assigned to you, which must be carried out within the policies and legal requirements of your organisation. As a customer service practitioner, you must be professional, flexible and good at communicating.

Scenario

Your colleague Frankie is going on annual leave. She has asked you to help her with a few tasks while she is away. In order to do this, you have to learn a number of new procedures. You chat to Frankie to find out what she does in the team and what her job responsibilities are. You find out that she phones customers and deals with complaints in a timely manner. Frankie prepares a handover for you, listing actions and people to contact. You work with her before she goes away, watching how she deals with customer issues and difficult problems.

Link

Module 1: Understanding the organisation (complaints or grievances)

Module 11: Personal organisation (dealing with customer conflict and challenge)

Activity

Job role responsibilities

Summarise:

- Frankie's job role
- the job role of a person in your department who has a different role to you.

Include each individual's specific responsibilities.

As a customer service practitioner, your job is to understand how the complaints process works and the steps you need to take to satisfy a customer's expectations. Chat to colleagues to find out how they handled refunds and the provision of replacement goods.

Customer complaints tend to occur through misunderstanding or as a result of being passed to another person. Listen to customers, show them respect and be professional. If they complain about a product or service, take notes and be sympathetic to them. If you are not sure what to do, explain that you will find a line manager to help. Observe how the line manager deals with the situation.

Link

Module 1: Understanding the organisation

How should you deal with complaints?

Activity

Dealing with complaints

Complete the step-by-step questions to check your understanding of how to deal with complaints.

Step 1

When dealing with a complaint, what do you do first?

Step 2

What information do you need to know from the customer?

Step 3

To whom do you report the complaint if you cannot handle it yourself?

Improve how you work by making notes or lists of what you need to achieve during the day. Highlight urgent or priority tasks to make sure they are completed in a timely way. Tackle emails at set times rather than spending all your time checking your inbox – this will give you the chance to concentrate on more difficult tasks that take time. Track your achievements, perhaps using a database or log to show productivity and goals achieved. If you fall behind, chat to colleagues to find out how they make best use of their time to complete tasks.

Summary

- As you settle into your department, you will understand more about your job role and your responsibilities.
- As a customer service practitioner it can take a few months to feel confident with the job.
- Take an interest in team members and their roles, and how the department functions. If you need help, ask for support.

Know the targets and goals you need to deliver against and how your actions impact on others

Key terms 

Target – an objective to work towards.

Goal – an aim or desired result.

Everyone in an organisation has **targets** and **goals** to meet and these must be achieved in a timely way. Each member of a department has their own goals, from the senior management team down. If you do not achieve your targets, this could drive down performance levels, reduce productivity and affect profits. Targets help an organisation succeed.

Setting targets

Within your own role, set yourself a target to achieve some key goals by the end of the week. A target could be to arrive ten minutes early to work; a goal could be to learn a new skill by the end of the day. Use planning tools such as mind maps to help plan your time and achieve your goals. The benefits of mind maps are that they help you to focus your thoughts by turning them into actions.

Mind map planning

Mind maps are planning tools that can help you to improve your workflow and organise your time. Look at the mind map in Figure 1 about improving target setting. Check what you know and are confident with. Reflect on what you are unsure of – these are the areas where you may need support or training. Discuss any points with a colleague or your line manager.

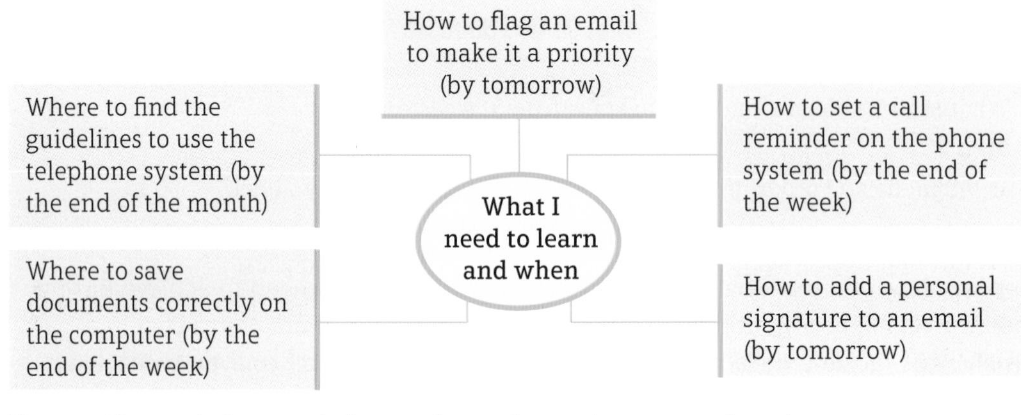

Figure 1: Use a mind map to help you plan and organise your work or time

Activity

Planning your time 1

Look at the mind map in Figure 1, then create one of your own that is specific to your job role. Use your mind map to find out if you are meeting your organisation's expectations and managing your work activities effectively. Can you tick off any of the targets and goals?

Think about the importance of each target or goal: what is a **priority** and what is most **urgent**? Agree priorities with your line manager and discuss any problems that might prevent you from achieving your targets, for example not having the correct piece of equipment to perform a task.

Key terms 

Priority – something that is more important than another.

Urgent – something that needs immediate attention.

Scenario

Hanna wanted to be more efficient at work. She talked to her colleagues to get ideas on how to achieve her targets. Then, she wrote a daily list of tasks to be completed, rating them from 1–5 under 'Urgent', 'Priority' and 'Can wait'. She added meetings and jobs to her calendar, and set reminders for tasks that needed completing in order to allow time to work on them. She flagged emails, set call times to phone customers and checked her list at the end of every day to see how her workload was improving.

Activity

Planning your time 2

Do you:

- plan your time to achieve tasks every day?
- use a calendar to plan your workload?
- rate tasks so you know what is urgent and what is a priority?
- plan resources to help achieve your goals?
- check daily on what you did not manage and set it as an action for the following day?

How could you better organise your time to be more efficient and achieve your goals at work?

How your actions affect others

Scenario

Elias was not enjoying his new job. He didn't get on with the team or his line manager. He preferred to be in bed, but his mother insisted he get a job, earn some money and get out of the house. Elias missed several deadlines for individual work targets but he didn't care. At the monthly team meeting, targets were discussed. His department had fallen behind on key performance objectives. This meant no-one in the team would get the bonus payment for meeting deadlines. Elias realised that his lack of care had affected other people. He had missed a bonus and was unhappy.

His line manager arranged a meeting to find out what was wrong with him. Elias had not realised how his lack of work would affect the team. His line manager advised him that, unless he tried much harder next month, he would be on a warning. He might even lose his job.

A poor work ethic and low performance affects the wider team, creating negative feeling. If you fall behind with work objectives, this affects productivity in the department and overall organisation.

All departments in an organisation rely on individuals working hard to meet their targets. Meeting targets leads to productivity and profit. An organisation cannot survive if its employees are not loyal or hard-working.

Activity

Logging work tasks

Collect data on tasks you do at work. Think about:

- how many phone calls you dealt with
- how many customers you were able to add to the database
- how many payments you took.

Try to log ten tasks, then compare the data week by week, increasing your figures so that you become more successful and can reach bonus payment targets. Collect feedback:

- from a customer you dealt with effectively
- about an occasion when you could have improved your responses when dealing with a customer.

When you have finished collecting your data, discuss your targets with your line manager. Show them the figures you collected on customer communications. Find out if your standard of work has improved.

1. What could you have improved?
2. What customer query could you have handled better?

Look at the sample hierarchy chart in Figure 2 showing lines of reporting in an example department.

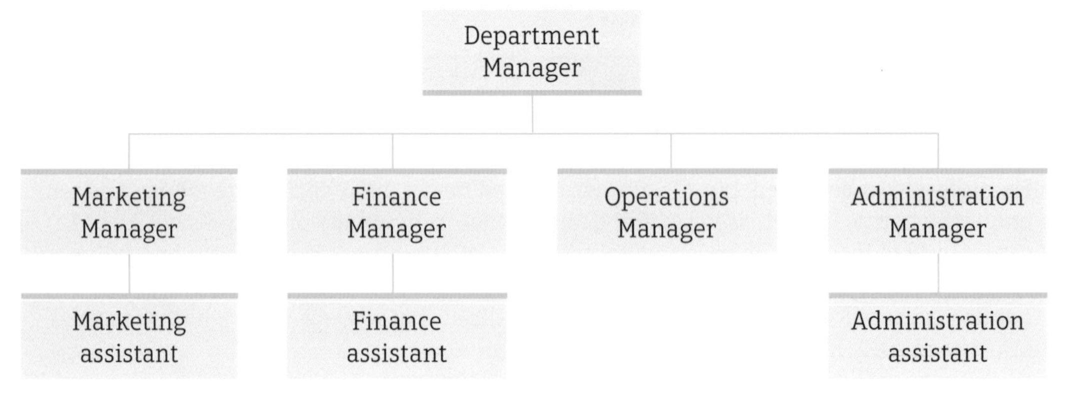

Figure 2: Hierarchy charts show the structure of an organisation

Activity

A hierarchy chart

To understand where you fit in your team, complete a hierarchy chart similar to the one in Figure 2 showing the members of your own department.

Professional working

If you cannot achieve your targets or meet the high standards in your department, your substandard work will affect the team. Poor customer service behaviour makes you (and your team) look unprofessional and does not meet expectations.

Discuss any concerns you have with your line manager. A colleague will be understanding, but your line manager will be able to help you or will find the right team member to help you. It might be that you need additional support with resources to achieve your goals. Or you might need more time to achieve your goals. Only by discussing targets with your line manager will you find out if you have the time and resources to achieve them.

It is better to be honest about what you know you can get done, than to fail at it. Your line manager will understand you better if you are positive and try hard. They have a responsibility to treat you equally and fairly, and to give you the time required to help you succeed in your tasks.

Try to improve your target levels. Be positive! If you are feeling overwhelmed, try and explain why to your manager.

Activity

Are you monitoring your targets effectively?

1. Did you:
- arrive at work early?
- use flags on emails (to remind yourself to follow them up)?
- talk to colleagues?

2. When communicating with customers, did you:
- demonstrate confidence?
- behave professionally?
- stay calm in a difficult situation?

3. Learning new skills
- Did you use new equipment or technology?
- Did you take charge of a situation and exceed your team's expectations?
- Did you handle information sensitively?

What could you do to improve the way you work to ensure you achieve your targets?

Summary

Reflect on your role in the department. Do you:
- feel confident dealing with issues and complaints?
- feel an effective part of the team because you are meeting your targets and goals?

Be positive: it takes time to learn new skills and behaviours.

The following activities will help you to strengthen the skills you have learned in this module about your role and responsibility.

Activities

Reflective account

- Have you completed the hierarchy chart to show where you fit in the department?
- Did you find out what your organisation's complaints procedure is?
- Have you observed how complaints are handled?
- Did you set yourself some goals to achieve each week?

Look back on the last month. Have your work goals and targets become more positive as your planning has improved?

EPA preparation

Summarise your organisation's complaints procedure in a short process chart to demonstrate what you have learned. You could use this chart to explain the process to a new employee or apprentice. Remember to add who to report the complaint to, where it should be logged and what details need to be written down, such as customer details, refunds, replacements, dates, and so on.

Behaviours

- Have you collected evidence on any training you attended?
- Have you tracked your goals on the mind map?
- Add a copy of your daily list to your apprentice showcase to demonstrate good use of target setting. If you collect a list from each month it will show how you have improved your target setting, as it becomes a more natural process. To develop this further you could put the information into a spreadsheet. Make it look professional by showing who you worked with on bigger tasks, adding dates for deadlines and adding colour to highlight priority tasks that need immediate attention.

4 Systems and resources

How do organisations use systems and resources to meet customer needs?

Organisations use a range of tools to manage service delivery. They use systems, equipment and technology to monitor delivery performance, using data to evaluate the efficiency of customer service delivery. In this module you will:

- learn how to use generic and bespoke systems, equipment and technology to meet your customers' needs
- understand which measurement and evaluation tools are available to monitor customer service levels.

Using systems, equipment and technology to meet your customers' needs

Organisations use systems, equipment and technology to meet customer needs. As a customer service practitioner, you need to find out what systems, equipment and technology your organisation uses. If you are trained effectively in how to use these systems, your knowledge and confidence will increase and you will provide a better experience for the customer. When a customer communicates with you, you will be able to provide the information quickly and professionally.

Key terms

Generic – a general product or brand with no copyright or trademark that is available for anyone to use.

Bespoke – something designed specifically for you, or for an organisation.

Telephony system – a system for making calls over the internet using computer software, hardware and network systems that provide the functions of a traditional telephone system. It is cheaper to run and can be used from any location with a computer and an internet connection. A traditional landline connects calls between two phones, limiting its use in larger organisations.

Systems

There are different types of systems in use in organisations.

- **Generic** systems provide a flow of information, from the first point of contact with the customer, to sales and invoicing.
- **Bespoke** systems are created for an organisation in order to meet their specific needs and processes.
- Marketing promotions and campaigns use customer data to target individuals, promoting events and new products or services.
- Data management systems provide information on productivity and customer interaction. Data can be evaluated and processes can be measured to improve customers' experience.

Organisations need systems to function efficiently. As part of your role, you will need to understand how these systems work. Here are some examples of the systems that a large organisation such as the National Health Service (NHS) might use regularly.

Systems in the NHS

Information and data helps health care professionals to provide better care to service users (those in hospital or being treated at home). Health care professionals in the NHS give the best possible care to patients, supported by customer service practitioners. As a customer service practitioner in the NHS, you might use:

- data management systems (for information on individual patients)
- security systems (for computer access log-in, or access to staff-only areas)
- prescription systems (for details of any regular medication that patients are taking)
- donor registers (for information about whether individuals have agreed to donate organs in the event of their death).

Customer service practitioners in NHS call centres book patient appointments using **telephony systems** that can:

- route calls
- log information
- link to desktop software with multi-channel communications
- use predictive dialling.

Calls might be channelled to staff with specialist knowledge. Calls might also be recorded to improve delivery techniques and most centres will use targets to improve responsiveness and sales.

Organisations such as the NHS use call centres to book patient appointments

Systems for delivery, performance and customer information

Scenario

Emma recently started work as a customer service practitioner in a call centre. During her first few months, she listened and observed how the team communicated to customers. She had training on the telephony system, using headphones to listen into calls, and finding out how to respond to queries and provide information. She made lots of notes, talked to colleagues about responding to demanding customers and started to understand customer expectations. She soon started to handle calls, transferring calls if she couldn't help, and was enjoying the interaction with customers. She was able to log information correctly and book customers onto events.

After she completed her **probation** period, her line manager asked if she would like to get bonus payments and they agreed to set targets on her performance. These were an **incentive** to work harder, as a reward for exceeding customer expectations.

Key terms

Probation – an initial period of time in which to see how a new employee fits into the organisation. The period can be extended if an employer is not sure how suitable the person is. Employees are only required to give one week's notice when in a probation period.

Incentive – something to provide motivation to do better.

Activity

Systems in your workplace

1. What systems do you use as a customer service practitioner to monitor delivery in your organisation?
2. Where is your customer information stored?
3. Complete Table 1 with the bespoke systems used in your organisation and how these meet your customers' needs.

Bespoke systems	How the system meets customer needs
What systems are used in your organisation to record customer information?	
What monitors performance?	
How are the systems used in customer service delivery?	

Table 1: Bespoke systems in your organisation

4. Are there any generic systems that your department or organisation use on a daily basis?

Link 

Module 2: Meeting regulations and legislation (GDPR)

Information may be stored on a customer relation management (CRM) system. This software might include linking customer queries to a customer database, or to marketing and financial information. Bespoke data systems are designed to fit a particular organisation's needs. Try to update information when a customer contacts you for information. Ask questions to check inaccuracies or missing information (ensuring that this is in line with data protection legislation).

Key terms 

Point of sale (POS) – combines software and hardware systems to take payment from customers for products or services.

Invoice – a bill itemising how much money is owed to an individual or organisation.

Self-service points – customers can scan and pay for items at a point of sale without the need for a member of staff.

Systems that use technology

All organisations use technology to monitor and manage customer information. Remember to record information accurately. These generic systems can be used by anyone. One such system might be **point of sale (POS)**, which works with most computer systems. This system provides receipts for customers and can send **invoices** to suppliers, and manage stock systems and sales data.

POS can work on a computer or a remote sharing system that backs up the data remotely. As a customer service practitioner you may use POS at a sales terminal to take payments from customers. The payment system may link to a register screen that the customer can also view (to check cost and quantity). It may also scan barcodes and link to the stock system to update you when stock levels need adjusting. The system may print a receipt or read a payment card. There may also be a secure place attached (such as a locked drawer) to store cash payments.

Your organisation may use **self-service points** to allow customers to scan and process their purchases. One disadvantage of these systems is that they cannot ask for identification (ID) if an under-age customer purchases items with age-restricted sales, such as alcohol. Customers like these systems as they reduce queues.

The advantages to the organisation are that they:

- are cheaper to manage
- are easy to train staff to monitor
- reduce staffing overheads
- speed up the sales process.

Some fast food outlets promote their menus on a self-service terminal but customer service practitioners are still needed to help those who are unfamiliar with the process.

Organisations that sell their products or services online will need to develop **web pages**. These contain text, images or graphics, and link to other locations. They might provide a link to an organisation's home page and allow customers to search for information. Advertising banners may promote other goods and services.

Think about any customer service practitioners that work remotely in your organisation. Do they use technology to share information? If they do, they will be using **telecommunications technology**. This includes communication systems such as the telephone network, radio broadcasting systems, computer networks and, of course, the internet. Information is transmitted electronically over distances by sound. This information includes voice calls and also images, text, video and data transfer.

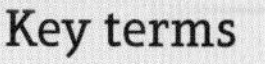

Key terms

Web page – these promote an organisation online and lead the customer to the information required.

Telecommunications technology – exchanging information using technology.

Organisations must stay up-to-date with changes in technology

Telecommunications networks might be internet-based, public, or radio and television networks. The better these networks work, the faster the communication they enable. Meetings can be held in virtual offices, with people collaborating via the internet.

Activities

What would you do?

Scenario

Lou was experienced in customer service, knowledgeable and confident talking to customers. One day a customer gave her some discount coupons at the till point. It would take ages to scan them and there was a big line of customers waiting to be served, so she called for help. Her supervisor opened another till point and asked the other customers to move to the newly-opened till.

Lou was happy to chat with customers, but she understood that some of them had limited time and needed to be served quickly.

- What would you do in this situation? Would you smile and ask the customers to wait while you scanned the coupons? Or would you get help to speed up the payment process?

The flow of customer information

1. Create a flow chart showing the flow of customer information in your organisation. Think about the following points:
   a. What happens when customers ask for information?
   b. What happens when customers purchase a product or service?
   c. What information is sent to customers regarding invoicing?
   d. How does the marketing department use information to promote new products or services?
2. Include the following points on your flow chart:
   - stock control
   - sales order
   - purchase order
   - marketing promotions
   - invoicing.
3. On your flow chart, show the area of work that you manage and any training that is provided on the system.

Remember to make your flow chart look colourful and professional if you want to show it to your line manager.

Your understanding of systems so far

What do you need to check when collecting information for a data system?

1. If customer information is inaccurate, would you:
   - make a note of what needs correcting?
   - ask the customer for up-to-date details when they next telephone?
   - make a courtesy call and ask to update their information?
2. How do you know if the information is current? Do you:
   - ask the customer to repeat unusual spellings on names, addresses, and so on?
   - check the customer's mobile number(s)?
   - check invoice references?
3. If you are busy and short of time, do you:
   - take notes?
   - make brief points with relevant information?
   - list points you need to ask the customer?

Equipment

Equipment that you physically use or touch could include:

- point-of-sale (POS) card readers
- self-service points
- card-swipe equipment used to pay a bill
- catering equipment such as pots and pans, or other kitchen equipment.

Technological equipment could include **smart connectivity** such as:

- mobile applications
- self-service availability
- SMS text support
- **live chat rooms**
- **support ticketing**
- **customer portal access**.

Smart connectivity allows controlled access to data applications such as smart technology in new residential houses, such as heating, security, sound, lighting and technology. Technology allows organisations to work more flexibly, for example employees can attend remote meetings using video conferencing applications.

Trade-specific equipment

Trade-specific equipment is developing all the time to speed up customer transactions for processing payment and delivery, for example hand-held order devices, card-swipe systems and catering equipment.

In the hospitality industry, for example, you might use a portable electronic POS. These reduce waiting time and the risk of incorrect orders as the orders are relayed directly to the kitchen. In addition, you can take payment on these systems without the customer losing sight of their payment card. Some terminals have a card-swipe facility; some have a pen for the customer to add a signature. Clever systems tell you if a dish is off the menu or could send a customer's dietary preferences to the kitchen. Customers get better service if you are not rushing around the tables. This, in turn, improves their dining experience.

This customer is using a wireless POS device.

Key terms 

Smart connectivity – where non-computers detect and analyse customer data, for example a refrigerator that recognises when you are low on food items, or a stapler that recognises when you are low on staples. Sensors are embedded into software applications allowing data exchange between the product and the manufacturer.

Live chat room – a virtual venue in which people can chat about their common interests online.

Support ticketing – a service request from an end user asking for support.

Customer portal access – allows customers to set up their own access to your organisation, for example to a recruitment area.

Activity

Technology in everyday life

1. Think about the last time you ordered food in a café or restaurant.
    - Did staff use a hand-held device to take your order?
    - Was a hand-held device used for payment?
    - Did it speed up the ordering and payment process?
2. Think of the last time you made a purchase in store.
    - Were there self-service points available to use?
    - Were there 'tap' contactless payment points?
    - If there was a conveyor-belt system, did you queue or use the self-service point?
3. At work have you:
    - attended a webinar meeting?
    - used technology at the meeting?
    - been given technology training?

Office equipment

Office equipment refers to the computers, printers and phone systems that you need in order to run an office effectively.

Activity

Starting a business

What equipment will you need? List your answers in Table 2. See if you can identify five pieces of office equipment, then give a reason why each item is important.

Office equipment needed	**Purpose of item**
1.	
2.	
3.	
4.	
5.	

Table 2: Items you would need to start up a business

Technology

Businesses use technology to check current information so that they can remain competitive against other businesses. Computer software enables them to manage information more efficiently. Stores use point-of-sale (POS) technology to take payment from customers. These are portable hand-held devices that allow customers to use swipe cards to pay for goods and services. Systems such as PayPal have accelerated payment systems for businesses. Hand-held devices are commonly used in lots of front-of-house areas to take customer payments quickly and promptly.

Technology has reduced the need for organisations to hold large quantities of stock, by introducing automated stock control systems that respond quickly to customer needs and online retail. For example, certain seasonal products are stocked in greater quantities at particular times of the year, such as charcoal for summer BBQs, and Brussel sprouts and turkey at Christmas.

Activities

Technology in your organisation

1. What is the most important technology used in your organisation?
2. How has this particular technology improved the way in which you do your job?
3. What are the benefits of using technology in general?

Become familiar with new systems, technology and equipment

Discuss the benefits of using new systems, technology and equipment as they are brought into your organisation with your line manager to understand how they affect you.

Summary

- All organisations use systems, technology and equipment. You may, however, use only a small proportion of the systems or equipment available at your organisation.
- Some departments will use specialised systems. Although you may not need to understand them for your role, it is helpful to be aware of them (especially if you enjoy using technology). As a customer service practitioner, it is important to find out as much as you can about your organisation. You can also look for roles in the organisation that you might like to progress into.

Understand types of measurement and evaluation tools available to monitor customer service levels

It is important that organisations monitor customer service delivery so that they can identify problems, make improvements and achieve their organisational goals.

Some organisations monitor customer service deliveries using QR codes

Key term 

QR code – a quick response (QR) code is a barcode containing information that can be read by smartphones; you scan the QR code in a book or product and then watch a linked video on your phone.

Link 

Module 1: Understanding the organisation (customer feedback)

Module 10: Influencing skills (customer feedback)

Monitoring and measuring customer service levels

Most organisations monitor customer service delivery:

- by asking questions, using phone apps, and via email and after-sales-service (informal feedback) surveys
- using rating systems
- through online customer surveys and face-to-face interviews (formal feedback)
- to assess complaints (refunds, or damaged goods)
- through recommendations to friends and family
- through social media activity, which can be measured by monitoring activity over time on social media platforms to provide data on, for example, marketing promotions
- using **QR codes**.

Why is it important to monitor and measure customer service levels?

It is important for organisations to find out whether their service delivery is running smoothly, and if there are any opportunities to improve their processes. Customers expect service to be professional and efficient, therefore standards must be maintained to ensure customer loyalty. As a customer service practitioner, you are essential in:

- maintaining customer satisfaction (identifying problems before they escalate into complaints)
- protecting the brand promise (to make sure that customers return)
- achieving your organisation's goals and targets.

You should understand your organisation's mission and values in order to promote their brand and encourage sales. An organisation's goals are to meet its mission statement and achieve a profit. If customers are happy with communication from the customer service team, they will buy into the brand promise.

Scenario

Yusuf was having problems settling into his new job in a reservation office. After the initial training period, his line manager was asking for improvements and had extended Yusuf's probation period. This upset Yusuf – he thought he was performing well. Yusuf's colleagues offered constructive advice by listening into calls with customers, commenting afterwards on the conversations and offering hints on what to say or write down.

Yusuf chatted to another new employee, Elena, about how he was feeling. Elena also felt she was being watched and that her mistakes were being discussed. She too had had her probation period extended. They knew each aspect of the job was measured, for example how many calls were answered, their duration (how long the calls took) and what the conversion rate of a lead call was to payment. They decided to turn a negative feeling into a positive one by measuring the data. The data used to measure team activity would show their line manager that they were aware of time management, deadlines and productivity rates.

Two weeks later, both Yusuf and Elena felt more positive about their rate of work. They had settled into the job and understood the products and services better. Their line manager was pleased and gave positive feedback on their performance.

Activity

Monitor service levels

Monitor service levels in your area to ensure that it is running properly and you are prepared for every eventuality at work. Think about the following questions in relation to your job role:

1. How many queries did you have from customers?
2. How many new customers did you speak with?
3. How many leads converted to a sale?
4. How many customer complaints did you receive?
5. How many returned or damaged goods did you deal with?
6. How much time did you take for each transaction?

By considering each transaction in this way, you can check how effective you are in your role and where you might need training and development to improve an aspect of your work. How can you improve your customer service delivery?

Evaluation tools to monitor customer service levels

The purpose of evaluation is to:

- measure and evaluate staff performance
- identify areas for improvement
- measure and evaluate customer satisfaction.

Evaluation tools provide data that can be used to monitor customer service levels, from the length of time it takes to answer a phone, to taking an order and processing payment. Organisations monitor and evaluate customer information to identify any problems in the service chain. Customer retention depends on the service you provide, on your knowledge and on how you present the brand, so it is important to identify any problems.

Importance of branding

You must buy into your organisation's brand image when dealing with customers and consistently provide an excellent service. Satisfied customers stay faithful to the brand and return to make repeat orders, using the products and services offered by the business. If an organisation fails to provide good customer service, customers will not return and may complain to friends and family.

By examining and evaluating areas of success and failure, organisations can check that their monitoring processes are effective. This helps to protect the brand: any areas of weakness can be improved through training. Training improves both employee knowledge and customer satisfaction, and strengthens the employer–employee relationship.

Customer service practitioners provide the service customers want and, in turn, receive job satisfaction from happy customers.

Evaluation tools

Look at the mind map in Figure 1 to see different types of evaluation tools. You might have some ideas of your own to add.

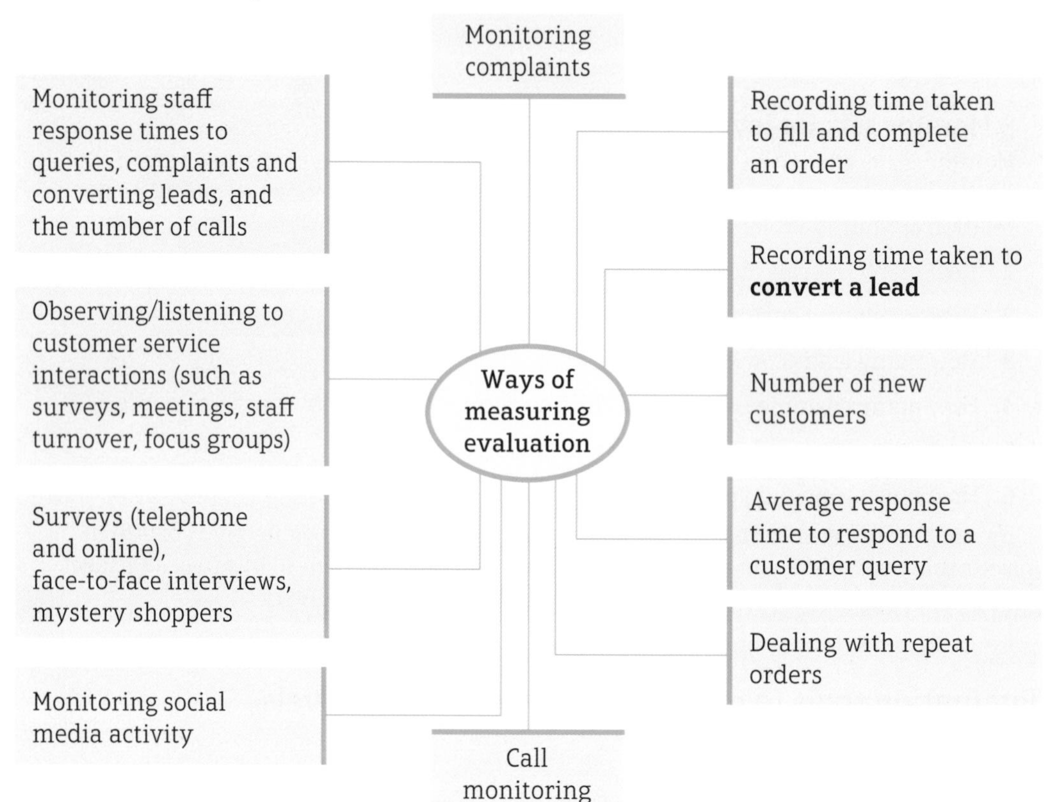

Figure 1: There are various tools you can use to evaluate customer service

Key term

Convert a lead – the process of changing a new contact into a lead or an opportunity for a sale. In a call centre, customer service practitioners will have targets for converting leads into new accounts, and must then promote features and benefits to the customer in order to achieve a sale.

Activity

Using the phone at work

1. Reflect on the last time you spoke to a customer on the phone at work. Were you:
   - professional on the phone?
   - knowledgeable about the products and services?
   - able to answer the phone without following a script?
2. When you communicate with customers, can you:
   - answer customer queries?
   - transfer calls?
   - understand specialist terminology?

Professional working

Customer service practitioners must be able to respond quickly to new situations with customers. Ensure you can provide up-to-date organisational information on products and services to customers and try to have a few key USPs (unique selling points) to hand. Assess your role in your organisation over a period of time, to see what is working well and not so well. Ask customers for their opinions to get first-hand information on anything that needs improving. Evaluating your practice helps to improve your customer service delivery.

Writing surveys

Surveys are useful evaluation tools for finding out information from customers. Discuss with your line manager how to organise a survey in order to get useful results. If a customer is not satisfied with the brand it might be because of a bad experience with a refund or replacement. Remember that the customer is influenced by a positive interaction with you, so make sure you are professional and helpful when resolving any problems.

It can be difficult to write surveys; it is important to plan them carefully. First, decide on the purpose of your survey. Remember – in a survey, you are trying to gather **qualitative** information from the customer that you cannot get from systems and data (**quantitative** information).

Table 3 will help you to understand the priorities for a survey.

Purpose of the survey	Questions
What do you want to find out?	Use open questions to focus on what you need to know. Open questions invite detailed answers; closed questions invite 'Yes' or 'No' answers.
Start with the end objective	If you understand the purpose, you can set the questions in order to get the desired result.
No leading questions	Questions should be **impartial** and not **biased** towards your organisation.
Gather results	The data will show you what customers want, what to provide and what products they are interested in. This helps to plan changes.

Table 3: Priorities when constructing a survey

Key terms

Qualitative – often expressed as an opinion or type using our senses.

Quantitative – data that you can count, usually expressed in numbers.

Impartial – treating everyone equally; not being too involved in a situation.

Biased – having a preference for a purpose or thing, and favouring that person or thing.

You can measure data gathered from the survey by 'ranking' or grading the questions. Questions may be ranked on a 1–5 basis, with 1 as 'most important' and 5 as 'not committed'.

Good data will allow you to plan and/or improve a process. For example, if a store has a high volume of returned goods and it takes a long time to process them, extra members of staff will be needed in that section during busy periods. Keep customer survey questions short, simple and to the point, perhaps only including three or four questions overall. Written or online surveys tend to focus on identifying satisfaction levels, underlying problems or improving a process.

The following are types of questions you might want to ask your customers:

- How well did our product/service meet your needs?
- What are the most valuable features for you?
- What would you change about the product or service?
- How would you rate its value for money/quality?
- How quickly were your queries dealt with?
- How easily could you find things on the website?
- What would encourage you to buy from us again?

To encourage customers to complete a survey, you could offer a reward or incentive (for example, a store voucher). This reinforces customer loyalty and encourages the customer to return to the store. Sometimes customers are happy to provide feedback; on other occasions they may not have the time. Do not be put off if a customer does not want to complete the survey for you – not everyone you ask or contact will respond.

Key term

Mystery shoppers – people who measure the quality of service, or gather specific information about a product or service for an organisation.

Mystery shoppers

Online surveys may be conducted by **mystery shoppers** to monitor customer service. Mystery shoppers look at market research on trends and behaviours, and provide reports on their findings to management.

Mystery shoppers provide unbiased information. They must have good memories in order to recall details of conversations and their observations before reporting back. As part of their work, they evaluate a service, looking at service quality and focusing on any areas for improvement.

Mystery shoppers might be involved in:

- store training
- evaluation visits
- telephone evaluation services
- online shopping services
- market research
- employee training.

Mystery shoppers will rotate to different locations so that they do not return to the same store too often. Sometimes they film their visits or monitor service at till points.

In these circumstances, it is important for them to make sure they are not noticed by staff. The purpose of mystery shoppers is to provide impartial information on service delivery. They are part of a good business strategy.

They will also check how the organisation is viewed by the public, highlighting problem areas and turning them into positive service areas for the customer. Customers stay loyal to an organisation if they are happy with the service. Without them, there is no business.

Mystery shoppers provide unbiased feedback on customer service

Summary 

- By now, you should have a better understanding of the importance of measuring and evaluating customer service levels.
- You may have designed a survey or be thinking of developing one. If not, it is good practice to write one.
- If you can see how to improve a process in your area, discuss your ideas with your line manager. This shows that you are taking an interest in the job and staying loyal to the organisation.

The following activities will help you to strengthen the skills you have learned and used in this module about systems and resources.

Activities

Reflective account

1. Think about the tools you have studied that monitor, measure and evaluate customer service levels.
2. What do you think about these different tools?
3. How have they helped you in your job role?
4. Are there any changes you would make to improve the monitoring process?
5. What would you need in your job to be able to make this improvement?

EPA preparation

A simple way to monitor how individuals in your organisation are working is to carry out peer observations. Staff observe an individual, away from their work area, to see how effectively they work. If you do this with a colleague, look for the following things:

1. Observe your colleague.
   - Are they friendly?
   - Are they smiling?
   - Are they paying attention to customers?
2. Does your colleague:
   - welcome customers as they approach?
   - make customers feel valued?
   - start to make notes of the conversation?
3. Does your colleague:
   - ask open questions to find out what the customer wants?
   - use information provided by the customer to up-sell products or services?
   - record information?

Chat with your colleague afterwards to see if they were aware of you making notes. Ask them to observe you at another time and compare notes. Their observations will help you improve your communication with customers and team members. Write the results of your findings in your apprentice showcase.

Behaviours

Consider what you have learned since starting at your organisation. Think of any skills you have gained, plus any new experiences. Add this information to your apprentice showcase.

5
Product and service knowledge

What product or service does your organisation offer?

Good customer-focused organisations need staff who are confident in their knowledge not only of the products and services on offer, but also of delivery services and post-purchase support. As a customer service practitioner, you should know what products and services are available so that you can keep up to date with what your organisation promotes. In this module you will learn:

- what products and services are
- the difference between providing a product and providing a service
- how to explain the difference between the features and benefits of your organisation's products and services
- how to keep up to date and maintain your knowledge.

What are products and services, features and benefits?

Customers may approach your organisation because they are searching for something in particular that they want to purchase. This may be either a product or a service, or a combination of the two. As a customer service practitioner you will promote or sell products and services to customers, or you may provide support in using them. It is therefore important you understand the features and benefits of the products or services your organisation provides, in order to give your customers informed choices.

Key terms

Product – an item that is offered for sale at a cost.

Service – a system, such as a transport or communications service, or the act of helping or working for someone.

Features – the important parts of a product.

Benefits – how a product or service helps someone.

Every organisation communicates about its **products** or **services** through advertising and promotion. You should be aware of launch dates, marketing materials and delivery arrangements. Find out about post-sales services too. Does your organisation provide a delivery service? Is technical support available for that new computer the customer has recently purchased, for example? Customers might want specialist support if there is a problem or they may want more information after their purchase.

Your organisation may promote a range of products or services, from locally sourced goods to items from across the globe. Your department may be responsible for several ranges but you should be confident about communicating each range to customers, together with its **features** and **benefits**.

Take, for example, a kitchen company's products and services. Examples of the features and benefits of each are shown in Table 1.

Products			**Services**		
Types	Features	Benefits	Types	Features	Benefits
Sinks, worktops, taps, doors, handles	Real hardwood doors, granite worktops	Long-lasting and durable	Kitchen design service	Virtual computer representations of what your kitchen will look like	Customers can accurately plan where cupboards would go, for example, so they end up with a design that works for them

Table 1: Example features and benefits of products/services provided by a kitchen company

There are organisations that only provide products (for example, cookers, hobs or mixed-control ovens) and others that only provide services (such as an electricity or gas provider) to support those products.

Link

Module 10: Influencing skills

Explaining the features and benefits of products and services

Let's look at an example. If a customer comes into the kitchen store you are working in, you will need to ask questions to find out what they want and how you can meet their individual needs.

1. Ask them about the product:
   - What type of kitchen are they looking for?
   - Do they want a fitted kitchen or a free-standing kitchen?
   - What design style do they want, for example open plan, modern, country style, traditional, central-island section, galley style, L-shape, French style, and so on?
2. Ask them about the features they might want:
   - What sort of work surfaces, seating arrangements, drawers for storage, corner cupboards, extending cupboards etc. do they want?
   - Do they want fixed or moveable storage units?
   - Do they need an organised area for storing pots and pans?
   - Do they want appliances to be included in the price and in the design?
3. Tell them about the benefits:
   - Fitted doors and drawers can be 'silent closing' to reduce noise.
   - Work stations can be positioned close to each other to allow ease of access and to save energy.
   - Good kitchen design should be easy to maintain.
4. Invite the customer to examine various styles of kitchen design. Use this time to chat in more detail about their needs, for example is the kitchen going to be a mixed-use family room or a sleek functional kitchen? If you show an interest in the customer, you can start to build a relationship and are more likely to get a sale.

Activity

Selling a product

1. Explain the features of a product you are familiar with.
2. How could you promote the benefits for a customer if you were trying to sell the product?
3. Explain the features of a service you are familiar with.
4. How could you promote the benefits for a customer if you were trying to promote the service?

Imagine you are promoting a product or service to a new customer. Use questions to find out what the customer wants, then explain the features and benefits in order to influence the customer to purchase the product or service.

Knowing your products and services

If you are familiar with your organisation's products and services, you will be more confident promoting them to customers. Attend product briefing sessions or external training, test the products and find out what the features and benefits are. Practise promoting them to colleagues to improve your sales knowledge. Demonstrate a product or service to a customer by asking them what they want, introducing the features and expanding into the benefits. When you are familiar with this information, try to **up-sell** or add an extra sale. An up-sell on a kitchen might involve getting a top designer to work with the customer to create their dream kitchen.

It might be hard to up-sell the first time you try it, but it increases profit margins. The customer has the option to take the extra item or to refuse it.

Key term 

Up-selling – encouraging the customer to buy something more expensive or in addition to the original sale, for example offering a customer a book of stamps if they buy envelopes, or a scented body lotion to complement a bottle of perfume.

Scenario

Adriana phones your organisation asking for several products. You greet her on the phone and make a note of her order. You are not sure if the products are in stock; you need to check their availability with a colleague. Select the best option:

- Option 1: Rather than keep Adriana waiting on hold, you offer to call her back with a price and delivery information.
- Option 2: You ask Adriana whether she minds being put on hold while you check availability, pricing and the cost of delivery with your colleague. You then provide the information to Adriana and take payment over the phone.

If you took option 1 in this scenario, Adriana may have contacted another supplier and purchased elsewhere by the time you call her back. Option 2 is the better option. It is important to have an up-to-date price list available, to check with a colleague on availability and to tell Adriana that the stock items will be posted out when the new stock arrives in.

Activity

Knowing your products

1. What would you have done in similar circumstances?
2. Would you prefer to wait while prices and delivery information were checked for you?
3. If you were the customer and the organisation did not have the information available immediately, would you shop elsewhere or would you wait for them to contact you?
4. If the organisation offered to call you back with the information within a given timeframe, would this make a difference to whether you waited or called someone else?
5. Would you be annoyed if the organisation did not have the information to hand to answer your request?

Knowing your customer

Scenario

Alex wants to purchase a new car. She visits a car showroom and talks to Jakub, a customer service practitioner. Alex explains that she is a regional sales manager and needs a car with at least four doors because she sometimes takes colleagues to team meetings at different office locations. She is happy driving a car with a larger engine and thinks a 2.0 engine would be fine as it would provide some power when driving but still be economical. Alex tells Jakub that she also wants leather front seats, electric windows and a sat nav. She feels it is essential to have a car with bluetooth connectivity so that she can keep in touch with the office.

Jakub is very helpful in promoting the features of a people carrier that has her choice of engine size and four-wheel drive. He tells her that it has a choice of leather or material seat covers, bluetooth connectivity and sat nav.

Once they have agreed the type of car, Jakub goes on to explain the benefits, which include comfortable seats for people doing a lot of driving, adjustable seat height to help getting in and out of the car, a large boot for storage, optional sun roof and air conditioning.

What were the features and benefits Alex needed in order to meet her individual needs? She knew she needed a reliable, economical car to transport her across her sales region. The car had to be comfortable, it had to allow her to communicate with the office and it needed to look smart. The benefits of having leather seats with back support and good IT systems were a bonus.

Different customers will have different needs when buying a car

Activity

Buying a car

Your needs might be different if you were buying a new car.

1. What influences you to choose a new car?
2. What would be your choices for features and benefits?

When promoting products or services, use the features and benefits to sell the item. Think about what would appeal to each customer based on their individual needs and preferences. Consider the different factors that might affect the sale. What makes a particular car appeal to someone, for example? Remember that customers might rank features and benefits differently from you (depending on their age, if they have a family or are single, for example).

Your decision about which features and benefits to emphasise will depend on a range of things from the cost of the product, to preferences for diesel, petrol, electric or hybrid cars, for example. You can turn features into benefits when promoting an item by using emotive language. If you can identify what your customer wants, you will more quickly move on to making the sale.

Activity

Features and benefits of a product or service

Copy and complete Table 2 with five features and benefits of a product or service in your organisation.

Product or service	Features	Benefits

Table 2: Five features and benefits of a product/service

Professional working

You can practise using features and benefits to promote products and services with your family and friends. You could also imagine you are a mystery shopper at another store in order to see how the customer service practitioner provides information on features and benefits to you. As you become aware of how to use features and benefits, you will start to use them automatically at work, raising your standards of delivery and sharing your knowledge with customers.

Updating your knowledge of your organisation's products and services

You should be familiar with the full range of your organisation's products or services. See Figure 1 for information on how to make sure your knowledge of your products and services is up to date.

Figure 1: It is important to stay up to date about the products and/or services your organisation offers

People see customer service practitioners as knowledge experts, trained to talk about the products and services in their organisation. You are there to provide expert knowledge to customers, and your customers trust both you and the brand.

As a customer service practitioner, you should have good knowledge of your products.

Activity

Customer service interactions

Think back to one of your recent customer service interactions. Did you:

- ask a few leading questions to find out exactly what the customer wanted to buy?
- demonstrate the item, introducing the features and benefits?
- let the customer examine the product?
- offer alternatives (in price and size)?

Updating your knowledge through training

As part of your role, you might receive training on new products or be given the opportunity to attend a 'customer event' promoting new products. It is important to attend such training sessions so that you are able to offer your customers the best product or service to meet their requirements.

For some customers, the best option might not necessarily be the latest product available. However, it is important to be able to offer customers as much choice as possible. After they have bought something, follow up by asking customers if they are happy with their purchase. Customers will value the opportunity to provide feedback and will feel satisfied that your organisation is following up the purchase. This boosts confidence for the customer and is likely to make them more loyal to the brand.

Summary

- It is important to understand the difference between products and services.
- Think again about the products and services that are available in your organisation and reflect on the differences between a particular product and service that you are involved with.
- Practice using features and benefits when promoting products or services to customers, family and friends. As you become confident with the differences you will find it easier to use them when promoting items to customers.

Maintaining product and service knowledge

In order to give customers a good impression of you and your organisation, keep up-to-date price lists and brochures to hand. This will ensure that customers have the right information available at the point of contact, which, in turn, will give them confidence in your products and services. Customers do not want outdated information or price lists – this appears unprofessional. Customers receive their first impression of an organisation when they walk into a store or view the home page of the organisation's website. If your organisation fails to update information, customers may wonder what else you are neglecting.

Selling products or services

If progress of a sale you are making slows down, offer the customer time to reflect on the item. This shows that you are not interested in a 'hard sell' but have time to listen to them and to wait. Provide customers with up-to-date marketing brochures, manufacturer manuals, price lists, service specifications or launch guides.

Link 

Module 1: Understanding the organisation (brand promise)

It is particularly important to keep prices up to date, as customers often look for reduced prices on annual discount days or at sale times. They may tell you that a similar store is selling at a reduced cost, to see if you too will discount the item. You will need to find out from your line manager how much discount you can offer.

You may need to refer your customer to a knowledge expert who can provide in-depth information on the development and history of a product. Customers enjoy hearing specialist information, especially when purchasing expensive products. Luxury consumer brands respond to customers who want a unique product made by craftsmen using one-off materials by allowing the customer to take part in the design process. Luxury car manufacturers, for example, allow customers to tailor their car to match their budget. Customers may be able to select the dashboard style they want or some of the internal features, such as seat cover colour.

Key term 

Warranty (or guarantee) – a written contract provided to the purchaser that promises to repair or replace an item within a given timeframe.

Some organisations offer **warranties or guarantees** as part of the after-sales service. The purpose of these is to increase sales.

New windows will often come with a guarantee of many years.

Sources of information

Figure 2 shows places to find information on a product or service.

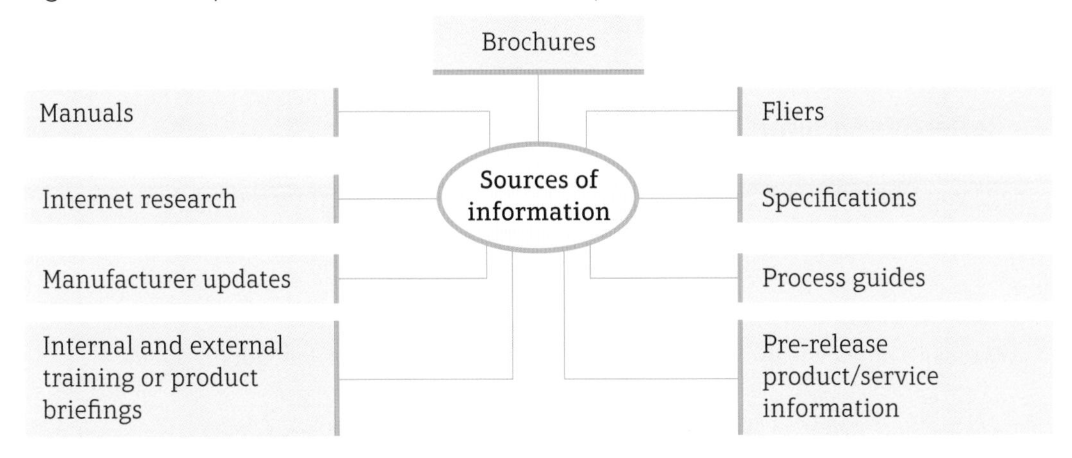

Figure 2: There are various places you can look for information on a product or service

To gain market knowledge, you need to know what your competitors are producing. You can build your commercial knowledge by being aware of what is going on in your industry, for example by finding out when a new competitor product is being launched and knowing how your organisation might respond with its own new products.

Customers are sometimes invited to special promotional events. These may be advertised on social media or just communicated to a select group of important customers. By inviting customers to a special event, you help to make them feel valued. It is part of the up-selling process and can be an extremely successful strategy.

What happens if you misquote the price to a customer?

Mistakes happen with pricing and are usually the result of human error. If an item is mispriced, the organisation can correct the cost at the point of sale. The customer must be informed that it is a pricing error and they can either pay the correct price, or not.

Offers

You might see '2 for 1' items for sale. Often items are marked up at a higher price than you would normally pay, but if the customer does not check that it is value for money, the organisation makes more money.

It is important to take care when pricing products or services, especially if items are advertised on the internet. The market is much faster moving and items are likely to be advertised to a bigger audience.

Summary 

- Your product and service knowledge inspires trust and respect in the customer, and helps to create a positive customer experience.
- It is essential that you understand the product features and benefits and ensure that you keep your knowledge current.
- Customers respond positively to someone who speaks confidently and with awareness about a product or service. Customer service practitioners who believe in a product sell it better than those who are disinterested in it.

The following activities will help you to strengthen the skills you have learned in this module about product and service knowledge.

Activities

Reflective account

Think about how your ability to communicate with customers has improved. What have you learned about promoting products or services? Record your thoughts in your apprentice showcase.

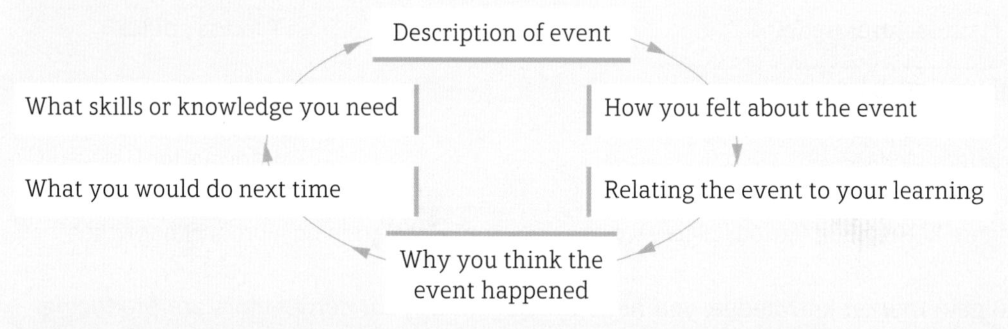

Figure 3: You can use the reflective cycle to help you reflect on your work

EPA preparation

By understanding the products or services available, you show that you have gained knowledge about your organisation. Over the course of one day, write down two things about each customer you come into contact with at work. Link an image to the individual to help improve your memory of something they said. This technique will improve your awareness of that customer's needs and build a good relationship with them for the next time they come into the organisation.

Personal development

Your business knowledge is improving daily. Check your knowledge of products and services when communicating with customers by reflecting on the amount of information you provide to them. Ask your line manager if you can attend training courses to learn about new products or services in your organisation. Add details of any training you plan to attend to a personal development plan (PDP) in your apprentice showcase.

6

Knowing your customers

Customer relationships

An important part of any customer service role is delivering excellent customer service.

In this module you will learn:

- who your customers are, and about their needs, priorities and expectations
- the differences between internal and external customers
- the purpose of customer service and managing customer relationships
- how to present a positive image of your organisation
- why it is important to be able to balance the needs of customers (customer service) with those of the organisation (brand and profitability).

You will also learn why it is important to treat customers equally and as individuals, and to accept diversity in every situation you come across.

Understanding your customers

You will come across many different customers in your role. It is important to understand who they are and how you should relate to them on a day-to-day basis. If you can understand and respond effectively to all customers, you will be a valuable member of the team. By doing a good job, you will also help to increase sales and your own job security.

What is a customer?

A customer is somebody who receives customer service from a service deliverer:

- Anybody is a potential customer once they enter or contact your organisation.
- Your customer base is the group of people who buy products or services from your organisation.
- Existing customers are people who regularly buy products or services from your organisation.

Types of customer

This section covers the types of customers you may come across in your job role and how to treat them.

Business organisations

Business organisations come in all shapes and sizes, and are a central part of our everyday lives. Your experiences of business organisations will vary depending on where you live. You will interact with them daily in very personal ways. You might use a coffee shop near your home or workplace to meet with friends or colleagues, or drop into your local mobile phone store with questions or problems.

Many companies have regular contact with other businesses who need their products or services. This contact could take a variety of forms from emails, phone calls or post, to large exhibitions launching new products or services.

Most business organisations fall into the following sectors:

- retail – stores selling directly to customers
- business to business – manufacturers supplying to retail organisations
- government organisations – offering services to a variety of different customers.

End users/consumers

An end user (or consumer) is any person who uses your product or service.
There are five types of customer you will probably meet in your job role.

Potential customer: **Potential Pedro** is not your customer yet – you will need to encourage him to buy your product or service. He has contacted you to make enquiries so he is clearly interested in what you are selling. You have the opportunity to convert, or change, that interest to a purchase.

Professional working 

- Show Pedro value – explain what he can get from your product or service.
- Promote yourself – make sure he knows that you are there to help.

New customer: New Nigel is a first-time customer who has just purchased something from your company. He is still learning about the product or service, so if you do not provide that help, he won't return or recommend your company.

Professional working 

- Guide him to success – Nigel will become a loyal customer if you take time to make sure he understands his purchase.
- Provide a contact phone number or email address for him – if he has a question later he will know where to go.

Impulsive customer: Impulsive Ihram is the type of customer who makes an instant decision to buy if the conditions are right. Ihram doesn't need much persuading; the fewer the steps involved, the higher the chances he will make a purchase.

Professional working 

- Clear the way to the checkout – make sure the information you give is uncomplicated.
- Provide quick and precise help – if Ihram asks a question, make sure you keep your answer short and avoid **jargon**. If it takes too long, his desire to buy will fade.

Key terms 

Jargon – special words or expressions that may be difficult for others to understand.

Discount customer: Discount Dave is the type of customer who knows the value of the product or service, but will never buy it at full price. He either wants extras for free or a discount. To make Dave a repeat customer, you need to show him that he is not only getting a great product but also the added value of exceptional customer service.

Professional working 

- Explain the deal – provide all the details so that Dave can make an informed decision.
- Offer added value – 'go the extra mile'. For example, before he asks, give him your name and work contact details, and explain that if he has any questions or needs more information, he can contact you directly. Be prepared to take responsibility.

Loyal customer: Loyal Laura is the type of customer who keeps coming back for more. She will contribute a lot to your company's income and will help your business grow. Laura will promote your product or serve as your brand's ambassador (be a representative for your business). She will provide positive feedback on the benefits of your business which you can use with other customers.

Professional working 

- Give her a platform – ask Laura to write a review on your website or social media.
- Keep Laura excited about your business – maintain regular contact with her.

Activity

Getting to know your customers

Think about any methods your organisation uses to get to know customers. What do these methods require you to do?

Key terms 

Commercially – in a way that focuses on buying, selling and making a profit.

Segmentation – dividing your customers into groups to identify their specific needs – this is especially useful for marketing purposes.

Different customer groups

Companies will not survive **commercially** if their marketing strategy (plan of action) relies on too broad a market. Market **segmentation** is important because it allows a business to target consumers with specific needs and wants. A market segment may be targeted through emails or relevant advertising publications. Segmentation helps companies to understand which customer groups are relevant to them.

Segmenting your customers into appropriate groups will help you to provide good customer service. This is because the types of customers using your service or buying your product will be in the marketing group targeted by your company. You will already be aware of what they need and expect when you deal with them. Table 1 will help you to understand the main segmentation factors in marketing.

Demographics (Statistics that identify different parts of the population)	**Geographic** (Cities, counties, regions or countries)	**Behavioural** (Lifestyle, buying and spending patterns, money and time)	**Customer value-based** (Benefits versus costs)	**Social status** (Class status of possible customers)
Age	Countries	Use of product and/or service	Revenue from customer	Economic situation
Gender	Cities	Knowledge and attitude to product	Costs associated with retaining customer	Lifestyle
Income size	Postal codes	Response to product		Activities
Occupation	Counties	Buying habits		Interests
Religion	Towns			Opinions
Race				Values and beliefs
Ethnicity				Personality

Table 1: The main segmentation factors in marketing

Activities

Types of customer

Can you think of any other types of customers? Add them to Table 1.

What do businesses need?

Think about the businesses that you have contact with.

You may deal with different businesses such as suppliers. Think about what they need from your company. List what your company provides for them and what they provide for your organisation.

Buying patterns

Buying patterns refers to the typical way in which we buy goods or services. Think about how often a product is bought, how many are bought, over what period of time and when (for example, toothpaste is usually bought when the old tube runs out). A good example would be an online weekly shop, where customers regularly buy the same brand of product because they are used to it, rather than out of loyalty to the store.

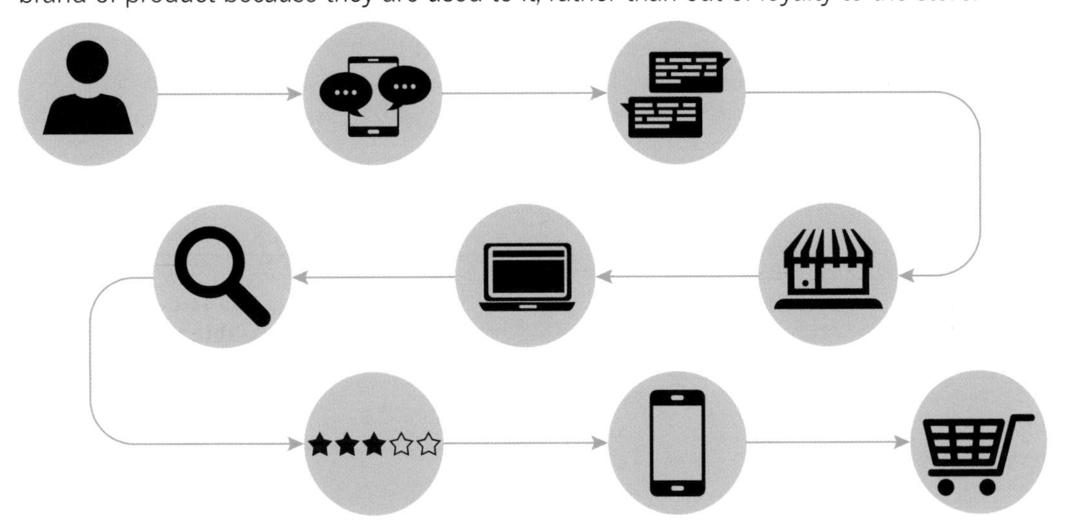

Figure 1: The typical way we buy goods or services is called a buying pattern

Activity

Buying pattern symbols

Look at Figure 1. Write down what you think the buying pattern symbols mean.

Regularly ask yourself these key questions:

- What are the customers' reasons for purchasing your product or service?
- How often will they need to buy that product or use that service? If you are aware of a customer's needs at the time you know they will purchase, the customer is less likely to look elsewhere for the goods or services.
- Who are they buying for? Your organisation's marketing and promotion will be dependent on whether they are purchasing for themselves or for someone else.
- Where are they most likely to purchase the product or service? If your customers say that they would prefer to order online and you do not offer that service, it makes sense to change the organisation's business model to include an online ordering service.

Summary

- Reflect on your role in providing customer service to different types of customer groups. Do you feel confident that you understand their needs?
- Maintain a positive and professional attitude and don't be afraid to ask a colleague if you have any doubts.
- Consider the use of segmentation in your organisation.
- Think about buying patterns in your organisation so that you can plan effective customer service delivery.

Benefits of building good customer relationships

Every business needs to develop good relationships with their customers. Good relationships will benefit the company because they will help to ensure customers' needs are met. This means they will be more likely to buy a product or service. Figure 2 shows the main benefits of building good customer relationships.

Figure 2: There are many benefits of building good customer relationships

Customer satisfaction

Customer satisfaction means that your customer is happy. To keep your customer happy, remember to do the following things:

- Give friendly face-to-face service – customers don't want to be greeted by someone who is bad-tempered.
- Answer customers' phone calls as quickly as possible – if you are busy on the switchboard, at least answer the call and politely ask them to wait. A customer will not be happy if they are kept waiting for someone to answer the call.

If a customer is happy with the service they have received and it has met their requirements, they are likely to feel satisfied. You can measure customer satisfaction using methods such as questionnaires (face-to-face or telephone calls), online surveys and customer focus groups (using social media to gather comments).

Customer retention

To be successful, organisations need to keep regular business from existing customers by providing the right products or services. You need to be aware of competitors' products so you can explain why your own products are better and so keep customers loyal to your company and your brand. Organisations should also develop ways of reducing the number of customers who leave.

The benefits of retaining your existing customers are as follows:

- It is five times cheaper to keep a customer than it is to find a new one.
- Loyal customers are more profitable as they spend more per order and will continue to spend.

- Your brand will stand out from the crowd.
- Existing satisfied customers will remain loyal and will give 'word-of-mouth' recommendations.
- Regular customers provide more feedback.
- Customers will be more likely to explore your brand.
- Loyal customers will welcome your marketing.

Activity

An angry customer

Scenario

A customer comes into your store – they appear quite angry. They explain that a product they bought recently does not appear to work properly.

1. What would be your first action?
2. How would you then deal with the situation? Remember the customer retention rules.

Customer recommendations

Existing customers who bought one of your products or used your service may write a review or make helpful comments about the company. Positive reviews can lead to increased business. Reviews will help new customers to buy a recommended product both online or in store if they are influenced by positive reviews.

Profitability

Although the words are similar, profit and profitability are not the same. Profitability is a measurement of the efficiency (effectiveness) of a company, and ultimately its success or failure. Profit means the amount of money a company makes when all costs such as production costs, marketing costs and taxes are deducted. If a company shows a profit at the end of the financial year, this doesn't necessarily mean that it is profitable. Retaining customers leads to profitability.

Increased sales

The final benefit of a good customer relationship is increased sales. If you manage your customers well, they will hopefully make more purchases, which will lead to increased profitability and growth of the company.

Summary

- It is important to make sure that your customers are satisfied with your service, so that they return and build up a good relationship with your business.
- This will hopefully lead to profitability and increased sales.

Understanding the difference between internal and external customers

An organisation has two forms of customers: internal and external customers.

Internal customers

Internal customers are the employees who work within an organisation or business. You will work with them to provide the best possible customer service. Everyone in the company is a customer to someone else. Internal customer service results in the ability (or inability) to provide excellent service experiences to external customers.

Remember – all of your colleagues are your internal customers. They expect to receive a quality customer service experience from you when required. For example, internal customers in a further education college might be:

- lecturers
- cleaners
- kitchen staff
- mini-bus drivers
- reception staff
- office staff
- line managers
- IT technicians.

It is important to keep your internal customers happy. People tend to think only of external customers – those people who purchase your products or services. Internal customers may not necessarily buy anything from you but each customer group has a large impact on the success of your business.

Imagine, for example, what would happen if you turned up for a skiing trip with a suitcase full of beach clothes? The trip would be a disaster and you would need to abandon it. The same applies to teamwork: everyone needs to know where they are going and to be well prepared for the journey in order to reach the destination together, with the right tools. You need to work together and be clear on your goals for dealing with customers. You need to consider both your own goals and how they link to the rest of the team, to make sure you can all work together effectively.

Activity

Internal customers

Scenario

Ayesha is a flower seller. She owns a flower shop and has recently come back from Covent Garden Flower Market with new stock. Jamie is a salesperson in the shop. He takes delivery orders and passes them to Jackie. Jackie is the flower designer. She creates a beautiful arrangement to fill the order and calls for pickup. Terry, the delivery person, picks up the order and delivers the flowers to the customer on time.

1. What would you do to make sure everything went well in this chain of events?
2. Can you think of something that may go wrong?

External customers

External customers are people who use your organisation's products or services. They are not part of the organisation, but have some connection to the business – for example, a customer who enters a store to buy its goods or services. In the example of the further education college, external customers could include:

- students
- suppliers (stationery, IT equipment, furniture)
- maintenance companies (plumbers, electricians, painters/decorators)
- mechanics (to service college vehicles)
- government organisations (for example, college inspectors)
- marketing companies (who supply logos or promotional material)
- catering contractors.

An external customer will expect value. They won't want to waste their money on a product that is not worth it, is overpriced or can be found more cheaply elsewhere. External customers provide a **revenue stream** that the company or organisation needs to survive.

Key term 

Revenue stream – a business term meaning sales or income.

Satisfied external customers are often loyal and make repeat purchases. They are also likely to refer your business to other people they know. On the other hand, if an external customer has a negative experience with your business, such as being treated poorly by a member of staff, this can also affect the company's success. The customer may pass on bad feedback to people they know. One person could tell up to ten other people about their negative experience; each of those ten could tell a further ten. You can see how one example of poor customer service could escalate.

Activity

Internal and external customers

1. Thinking of your organisation, give three examples of internal customers that you may deal with.
2. Again thinking of your company, give three examples of external customers.

Summary 

- We have looked at different types of customers both internal and external.
- It is important to understand who they are and the differences between them so you can meet the needs and expectations of each type of customer.

Managing internal and external customer relationships

It is important to understand how to communicate with both internal and external customers. They each have different requirements. Although your way of dealing with them will also be different, remember that you must always deliver excellent customer service to both groups.

These days, people communicate in many different ways. For example, by:

- letter
- email
- phone call
- text message
- social media site
- web call.

It is easy to overlook the importance of communication. When communicating with your internal and external customers, you must be sure that the message they receive is the message you intended to send. Otherwise you may be offending your customers without even realising it!

Clarity

As people increasingly use the written word to communicate emotions or ideas (often in 140 characters or less), there is a risk of being misunderstood. When communicating with customers, particularly in instant messages such as email or social media, re-read your message before pressing 'send' and consider what you are sending. Avoid too much detail in emails and clarify the purpose of the email to make it easy for the customer to understand. Always be specific.

Formality

Most modern business communication is polite but casual. Email is the most formal medium – unless you know the person well, start with 'Dear' and use their surname. When communicating with your external customers, make sure you sign off in a formal manner such as 'Kind regards' or 'Sincerely'. 'Many thanks' is perfectly acceptable for your internal customers at work. Social media, on the other hand, is less formal. Write like you speak and read it aloud. Ask yourself whether this is something you would say if the person was in front of you.

Activity

Clear information

Scenario

A customer from Italy comes into your business. He needs information on a product that he wants to take back to his own country. He wants more information about whether it is compatible with (suited for) Italian systems but is having difficulty understanding your explanation.

1. What could you do to make your explanation clearer for him?
2. If you were uncertain where would you get the information to avoid further queries from the customer? Remember, it's public!

Anyone can forward an email and tweets can go viral, reaching a large number of people in a very short time. Make sure that you always stay professional when communicating on company social media pages and websites. It is important to remember that you are representing your organisation and are responsible for its reputation. Look carefully when responding to messages to check you are not just giving your opinion. Double-check that the content is appropriate before pressing 'send'.

Face-to-face or telephone communication

Email is not always the easiest way to make contact. If there has been a misunderstanding, pick up the phone and speak directly to your external customer. Alternatively, see if they can visit your company. If you are communicating internally, go and see the person at their desk. Most problems are far easier and quicker to resolve when you can hear the person's voice or see their face.

When dealing with customers, either face-to-face or over the phone, it is important to think about your tone of voice. Speak slowly and clearly so they understand exactly what you are trying to say. It is a good idea to change the pitch of your voice when giving an explanation in order to emphasise a point, but remember not to shout. Think about the importance of body language and smile when necessary – even over the phone, callers can feel when you are smiling.

Activity

Good customer service

Remember – a key part of the customer experience is the helpfulness and responsiveness of the person communicating with you.

1. Can you define good customer service?
2. How do you respond to the customer?
3. What feeling – good or bad – do you think the customer has when they are talking to you?

Summary

- It is important to communicate clearly with both internal and external customers.
- Choose the best medium for communicating and always check your writing before you send a message.
- Be professional – remember that you represent your company every time you communicate.

Your company's policies and procedures

Companies provide customer service policies and procedures to give guidance on how best to serve their customers. It is important that you read and understand your own company's policies and procedures.

Key terms

Code of professional conduct – a list of company standards that staff should follow when dealing with vendors, customers and employees.

Protocol – unwritten rules, or guidelines, that should be followed in business dealings, and are usually learned in on-the-job training.

A customer service policy is a written **code of professional conduct** for employees to use when serving customers. It could include information such as how to respond to questions or deal with unhappy customers who want refunds. A policy can be short or it can be detailed. It may state what behaviour is expected when a certain situation occurs. It may also give details of appropriate steps for taking action. Typically, managers determine the policy and include it in the employee handbook.

A customer service procedure is a way of carrying out a routine practice. There is a **protocol** to follow in customer service in order to remain competitive. Finding a better or faster way of doing something can be considered a customer service procedure. Managers will evaluate your job performance to see how improvements could be made. This will lead to increased efficiency and better customer service.

What your company should do

Companies should look for new opportunities to improve customer service policies and procedures. Both employees and managers should look for new methods for helping and serving customers. If your job changes, your company should write new customer service policies and procedures to cover your new tasks. It is important that you understand what you need to do.

What you should do

You also have a responsibility to maintain customer service policies and procedures.

- Make sure that you read and understand your company's customer service policies and procedures.
- Be aware of how to treat external customers (those who buy your products or services) and the legal rights they may have.
- If you are required to deal with customer calls, make sure that there is a system in place so that they are answered immediately.
- Always apologise for putting a customer on hold when you return to a call.
- A customer service professional should be able to recognise immediately if they can help a customer, or if the customer needs to be transferred to a manager or a different department.

Activities

Your organisation's policies and procedures

Research your organisation's policies and procedures. Make sure that you read the staff handbook – this will provide you with essential information to do your job effectively, efficiently and professionally.

Options for your customers

- How do you find out what is best for your customer?
- What would you do to make sure that you have the correct information to help them?

Your company's customer service policies and procedures will give you guidance on how you should serve your customers

Summary

- It is important to understand and follow company policies and procedures.
- All companies, whether large or small, must have policies and procedures in place, as this is an essential part of customer service.

What is the purpose of customer service?

Good customer service helps to ensure that:

- your company makes a profit
- your company delivers services and products that satisfy and please customers
- your company gains a competitive advantage in your particular industry
- your customers develop loyalty towards your company and improve your company's reputation.

Good customer service is a way to build trust with both potential and existing clients. Satisfied customers will hopefully recommend your business, provide repeat business and increase chances of long-term success. Repeat business is considered a privilege and the service you provide should focus on creating personal connections with your customers in order to build loyalty. Customers who feel a personal connection to a business are more likely to share positive feedback with others and, in so doing, market the company. When customers are satisfied and feel special, they are more likely to tell their friends and family, ultimately increasing the customer base for the company without the need for expensive advertising and marketing.

Understanding customer wants and needs

Understanding the difference between what a customer wants and what they need is a major factor in succeeding in business. It is easy for a customer to confuse what they want with what they need. As a customer service professional, it is your job to give the customer what they want. Although you can help them to understand what they need, it is not your responsibility to convince customers to get what they need.

Businesses make money by satisfying their customers: it is often easier to sell them what they want than what they need. Focus on why they originally contacted your business – do not decide what you *think* they need (although you can advise them if you believe a certain product or service is more suitable for them).

Most people prefer to buy something rather than have it sold to them. There is a subtle yet important difference between the two. When people decide for themselves what they want and go out to get it, they feel like they have bought it. If a salesperson convinces them to purchase something (even if they need it), the customer may feel like the salesperson has persuaded them to do something against their will. If you want customers to feel good about the relationship and are interested in customer retention, you have to give them what they want.

Needs versus wants

Sometimes what a customer wants is not what they need. In this situation, share the information you think they need to know but allow them to make the right decision for them without feeling pressured. In some cases, the customer will agree with you, change their purchase and thank you for your help. In others, they may completely ignore what you say and pursue what they want over what you know they need. If you want to build a successful business, you must be willing to sell them what they want without making them feel uncomfortable about their decision.

What the customer wants is often a more powerful motivator than what they need. Ask them to tell you why they want what they want, then listen carefully to the answer. Usually they have a desire to get what they want and simply want you to show them how to get it. Customers tend to get more value, joy and satisfaction from purchasing what they want then what they need. Successful sales people understand this and know how to use it to their advantage.

Link 

Module 10: Influencing skills

What are the priorities for the customer?

Each customer will have different priorities when buying a product or a service. The main priorities for you are to:

- listen to what they have to say so you can understand what they really want
- understand their needs
- help them to avoid mistakes in their selection
- give clear communication so that they understand the purchasing process.

The average person is usually willing to spend more on what they want than what they need. For example, if a homeowner needs a new roof, they will usually look for the least expensive one that meets their needs. However, if they see a particular type of roof tile they want, whether they need that type or not, they may be willing to pay whatever it costs to get it. The purchase makes them feel good so price is not a barrier, as long as they can afford it.

Summary 

- It is important to understand how to give your customer what they want at a price they can afford.
- It is a lot easier to sell people what they want than what they need.

Customer expectations: actions speak louder than words

A customer expectation is what a customer assumes they will receive when they contact an organisation. Features of customer expectations include:

- product/service performance – what is good value for the money they are spending?
- good interpersonal skills from staff – to provide accurate and reliable information and advice on all aspects of the purchase
- clear communication – person-to-person relationships are extremely important in customer service and many customers expect this
- efficiency in the purchasing process – such as information on warranties in case of breakage or the best way to contact someone for help and advice.

Key term

Staff charter – document designed to provide staff with clarity and a shared understanding of what is expected at work, in order to ensure that they deliver high quality service to all customers.

Customers' expectations can vary depending on a variety of factors, such as an organisation's vision or mission. Organisations must have positive values and offer exceptional customer service in order to attract customers. They should also offer services based on values taken from the **staff charter** and a commitment to providing good quality products. Brand awareness and loyalty helps customers know what to expect. They see their chosen brands as reliable and meeting their needs.

Customers expect certain standards when they visit a business or an online store. You should understand how to identify, meet and exceed those expectations, in order to provide them with the highest level of service and to achieve customer satisfaction.

How can good customer service affect an organisation's success?

This process isn't necessarily straightforward. Customers expect:

- value for the money they spend
- clear and accurate information
- friendly staff with good communication skills
- to be treated as individuals, with their personalities taken into account.

Key term

Bottom line – how much money the company makes.

If you do not meet customer expectations, this can have a direct effect on your organisation's success and profits. Customers who receive excellent service will improve the **bottom line** of your organisation by returning for repeat business. Four out of five people are more likely to work with an organisation after receiving good service.

Quality of service

- Give exceptional quality service to encourage customers to return to your business. According to Right Now's *Customer Experience Impact Study*, 82 per cent of customers would stop using a business if members of staff were rude and incompetent, 18 per cent more than if their issue was not resolved swiftly.

- Demonstrate your knowledge of your organisation's products or services. You should be able to provide specialist advice and guidance on products, services and technical support.
- Provide additional services or information to customers once they have bought the product to meet customers' needs and contribute to your organisation's success. You can do this online, via help desk support, at delivery or after sales.

Connecting with customers

- Spend more time with your customer if you can. It is no longer enough to be friendly and efficient in solving customer enquiries; you have to connect with them too.
- Exceed a customer's expectations. Your most positive customer experiences are probably the result of a staff member doing more than was expected of them. In these cases, you are more likely to return to the company and buy their products.
- Customers expect to interact with an organisation in a variety of ways: telephone, email, online (website and social media). However, they still expect to receive a personalised communication, whichever method is used. You can promote your organisation by being knowledgeable, approachable and empathetic, so that customers feel they are being heard and helped with their enquiries.

Customer feedback

Customers generally expect and appreciate follow-up communications, promotions and advertising. The key is to give them the right amount of information at the right time through the channel they prefer. They must also be given the choice to stop the communication if they want.

You can use customer feedback to help you identify where you are treating customers fairly and where improvements are needed. Remember – a satisfied customer is not necessarily being treated fairly. Feedback helps to flag risks for you to consider. If you use customer feedback, think about the questions you ask. Ensure they help you to identify areas where your organisation can improve the treatment of customers.

Activities

Positive feedback from a customer

You have dealt with a customer who has provided positive feedback about the process and item purchased. Consider how and when you can use feedback to get the most from it.

A dissatisfied customer

It is not always easy to discuss issues with unhappy customers, If you have had a dissatisfied customer, discuss the reasons for their complaint. If not, check with a colleague and ask them how they dealt with the situation. Use the feedback to improve your service at your organisation.

Exceeding customer expectations

Think about customer service situations you have encountered. Did you go above and beyond the minimum customer expectations? List three ways in which you could exceed customer expectations.

Summary

- Customer service is not about telling people how great your organisation is or giving figures to prove it. It is about creating memorable experiences for your customers.
- Remember to take your time, connect with your customer and do more than they expect.

Knowing when to adapt your customer service to meet customers' needs and expectations

As a customer service professional, you should be able to use different approaches in different situations. You need to adapt the way you respond to customer needs according to the context of a situation. Different techniques work for different customers. It is essential to recognise how a customer would like to be treated from your first point of contact with them. You can then choose the most suitable approach based on your own experience and instinct. You also need to be able to balance the needs of the customer and those of your organisation.

Adapting your customer service approach

Being able to adapt the way you communicate with different customers will help you to:

- develop a rapport (a bond) with customers
- deal effectively with a variety of situations
- minimise the chances of misunderstanding, miscommunication or frustration on the customer's part. (It may be that there are certain customers you will struggle to communicate with. In such cases, seek support from your line manager.)

A successful business will adapt its customer service approach to meet its customers' needs and expectations. Examples include:

- providing excellent customer service – ensuring staff are knowledgeable, experienced and trained; ensuring employees look presentable, demonstrating a good personal attitude when dealing with all customers
- making sure there are suitable facilities for wheelchair users and people with hearing difficulties, such as hearing loops at enquiry windows
- offering additional services to meet customers' needs once they have brought a product or if they need additional information on the product – this can be done online, via help desk support, at delivery or after sales
- being flexible – an organisation could have flexible opening times to meet the needs of customers who cannot shop at certain times, or make more services available online
- having staff on-hand to deal with customer complaints both face-to-face and online – as more customers turn to Facebook and Twitter to air their complaints, businesses must pay close attention to social media so they can turn a bad experience into a good one.

Balancing the needs of your customer and your organisation

If organisations cannot balance customer expectations with their own business needs, they will risk having unhappy customers or they will lose profit. Customers now have the power to influence many other customers by giving positive or negative online reviews, so it is essential that organisations provide the highest possible level of customer service.

Effective customer service leads to customer loyalty, bigger spends, repeat business and brand recommendations. However, research by Harvard Management has revealed that while 80 per cent of the companies surveyed believed they were serving their customers well, only 8 per cent of their customers agreed that they received outstanding service. This is a clear indication that most organisations are unsuccessful in balancing customer expectations and business needs, and that good customer service is often neglected. Figure 3 lists the things you must know in order to provide excellent customer service.

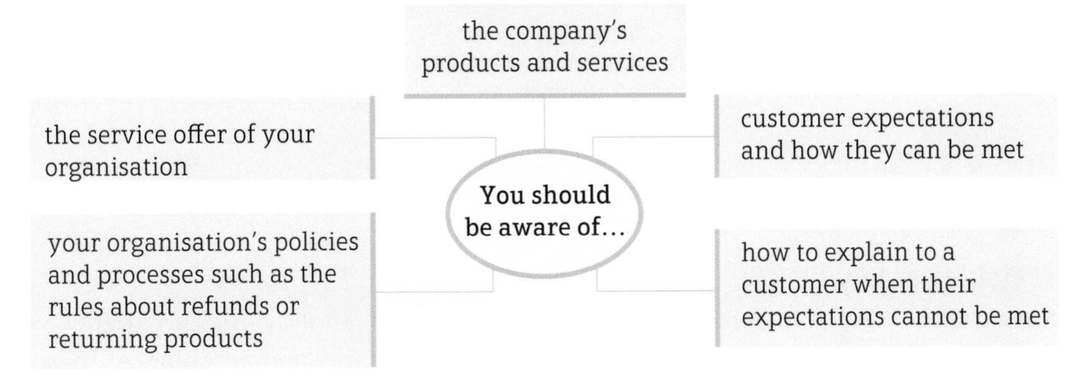

Figure 3: Essential knowledge for providing high levels of customer service

Summary 

- It is important to be aware of how your organisation can balance their own needs with their customers' needs.
- The balance between organisation and customer feeds into many aspects of customer service delivery and experience.

Responding to different customer types

As a customer service practitioner it is important to understand the different customer types you may come across. This will help you to adapt your approach depending on who you are dealing with.

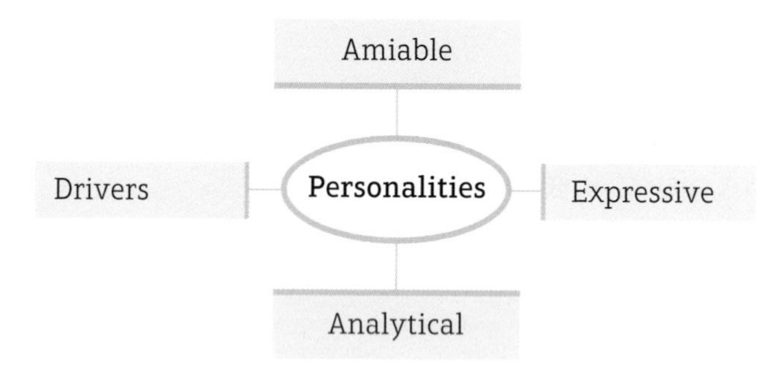

Figure 4: You can improve your customer service skills by understanding the different customer types you may meet

Amiable personality

People with an amiable personality are known for being friendly, supportive and focused on people. They value co-operation, personal security and acceptance. They respect other people's opinions and like to develop a relationship before conducting business. They usually reach a decision quickly, but need some time to build rapport. Being outgoing and social, amiable people enjoy working with other people in a team, rather than individually, and tend to focus on team results.

Your approach: *As customers, amiable people expect you to be considerate and friendly. They are likely to chat for a while before getting down to business. When providing customer support to people with an amiable personality, focus on why your product, solution or advice will meet their needs. They would also appreciate you sharing similar positive experiences from other customers.*

Expressive personality

People with an expressive personality are spontaneous, confident and enthusiastic. They enjoy involvement, excitement and creativity. Expressive people like to come up with new ideas, but they may not be able to see their ideas through to the end. They dislike details, and tend to focus on opinions and stories rather than facts and data.

Your approach: *As customers, expressive people tend to make slow buying decisions. They typically expect you to spend some time socialising with them before getting down to business. Once you get to the point, keep their interest by focusing on the big picture, and avoid spending too much time on details. Expressive people usually like to know who uses your product or service. They are more likely to buy products and services that are recommended by people they know – be ready to share your best testimonials.*

Analytical personality

This personality type is usually described as cautious and thoughtful. They prefer to make informed decisions and value numbers, statistics and details. They tend to appreciate formalities, standard operating procedures, organisational rules and predictable ways of doing things. When making their choices, analytical people generally aren't interested in what other people think. They prefer to rely on their own opinions and the facts.

***Your approach**: When you deal with analytical customers, give clear, detailed responses and use step-by-step procedures. Providing data, facts or instructions in a direct organised manner is the best way to support people with analytical personalities. Show them how your service or product will meet their needs. Use specific examples and let the facts speak for themselves. Be ready to offer background material and any research data they might need to make a decision. Then, give them time to consider all the facts.*

Drivers

Drivers have a dynamic and active personality type. They are confident and naturally tend toward leadership positions. They take action quickly and are not that interested in details. Drivers have a broad view of things. They have a clear direction, but they may not always take the necessary first steps to get there. They are independent and productive. A driver would rather make a bad decision than no decision: they simply want a decision to be made.

Drivers, however, can be insensitive, unsympathetic, harsh, proud and sarcastic. They do not like to admit when they are wrong. They can also rush into a decision without thoroughly thinking it through, or understanding the results or consequences of their decision.

Analytical people and drivers might not work very well together but their skills can complement each other. It has been said that if you want to get to the Moon you hire a driver, but if you want to get back again you hire an analytical person.

***Your approach:** If you feel that your customer may be a driver type, give them an outline of the facts to help them make up their minds. Then, allow them to arrive at their own decision. You are unlikely to get a comeback if they make the wrong choice.*

Summary

- Adapting your approach can be a difficult part of your role as a customer service professional.
- Identifying and understanding the motivations and communication styles of each personality type will help you to provide excellent customer service.

Fair treatment of customers

As a customer service professional, you must treat all of your customers fairly and understand how the Equality Act (2010) affects both your customers and your organisation.

Link 

Module 2: Meeting regulations and legislation

Legislation such as the Equality Act (2010) protects the rights of individuals and ensures equal opportunities for everyone. While 'equal' does not mean that we are all the same, and it is important to remember that each of us is unique, we do also have common qualities that make us all human. This means that every individual should be treated with respect and dignity, and we should treat others in the same way.

Legislation controls the services that you provide, ensuring that they are carried out with reasonable care and skill. Any information you give to the customer, either verbally or in written form, is legally binding. Services should be offered at a reasonable price and within a reasonable time scale.

Organisations should aim to achieve the following six outcomes to ensure fair treatment of customers:

- **Outcome 1:** Customers can be confident they are dealing with organisations where fair treatment is central to the organisation's culture (values).
- **Outcome 2:** Products and services marketed and sold in the retail market are designed to meet the needs of customer groups and are targeted accordingly.
- **Outcome 3:** Customers are provided with clear information and kept appropriately informed before, during and after the point of sale.
- **Outcome 4:** Where customers receive advice, the advice is suitable and takes account of their circumstances.
- **Outcome 5:** Customers are sold products that perform as organisations have led them to expect. Any associated service is of an acceptable standard and as they have been led to expect.
- **Outcome 6:** Customers do not face unreasonable post-sale barriers imposed by organisations to change product, switch provider, submit a claim or make a complaint.

The flow chart in Figure 5 demonstrates the potential consequences if you fail to follow equality legislation.

Reason

This could be a dispute taking place. The customer feels that they are being discriminated against due to age, race, religion, gender or sexual orientation.

↓

Consequence

Breaking the code of conduct could result in diagreements and arguments in the organisation.

Not only will this cause disputes but the reputation of the organisation could be damaged. Staff could leave causing overall understaffing. People may not apply for available positions because of the organisation's reputation.

↓

Result

The end result could be that the company closes down because they are not making a profit.

There may be legal action involved depending on the degree to which the customer felt they were mistreated. If the issue is very serious, you could be prosecuted. This could mean the organisation is fined or even taken to court.

Figure 5: A summary of the potential consequences if you fail to follow equality legislation

Activity

Equality legislation

Explain how equality legislation affects your customer service role.

Summary

- It is important to treat all customers equally – it is an essential process in the delivery of customer service.
- It is also important that you understand how equality law affects your organisation.

The following activities will help you to strengthen the skills you have learned and used in this module about knowing your customers.

Activities

Reflective account

Look back at the section 'Knowing when to adapt your customer service to meet customers' needs and expectations' on pages 80 and 81. Use the reflective cycle in Figure 6 to describe what you have learned.

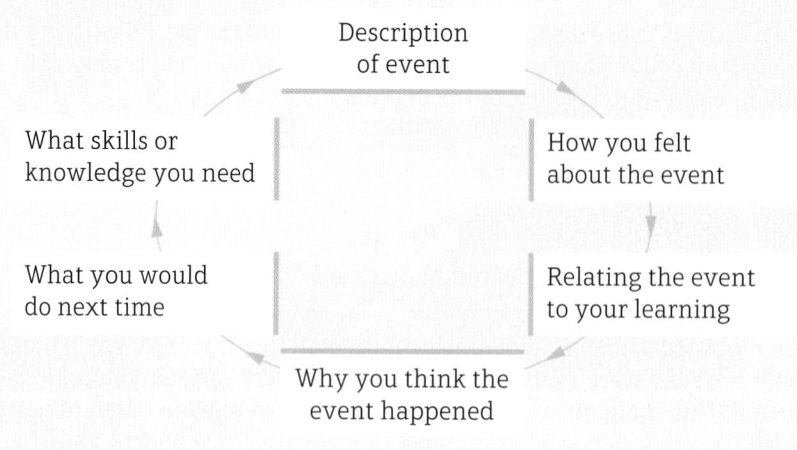

Figure 6: The reflective cycle

EPA preparation

How would you adapt your approach when dealing with internal and external customers?

Look at how you would deal with:

A. internal customers

B. external customers.

Draw up different questions which you could use to gather information about needs and expectations.

Behaviours

How would you describe good customer service?

What does exceptional customer service mean to you?

What would be effective behaviours to understand customer needs?

7

Customer experience

Making customer service memorable

The 'customer experience' encompasses a customer's first contact with you, how you deal with their enquiries, how you conduct yourself, their impression of you and your organisation, and their ultimate satisfaction with the products and services.

In this module, you will learn about how to:

- create a customer-focused experience
- build trust with customers and why this is important
- deal with potential conflict and challenge
- treat customers as individuals.

What is a customer-focused experience?

'Customer-focused experience' is a marketing phrase that means keeping the customer at the heart of the service culture when selling products and services. Customers have particular needs and wants; you and your organisation must meet these in order to increase sales and profits. Some organisations structure their management teams around specific types of customers, for example individual consumers or businesses.

Link

Module 5: Products and service knowledge

How to create a customer-focused experience

Know your product or service

To provide good customer service you need to make sure you:

- have an in-depth knowledge of what you are selling
- know how your products or services work
- anticipate the most common questions that customers may ask and have appropriate answers to hand. Your aim is to make sure that customers are satisfied that their queries have been answered.

Link

Module 9: Interpersonal skills (open and closed questioning techniques)

Ask questions to understand your customers' needs and expectations

Use open and closed questioning techniques to gather information from customers in order to establish what they want and need. This will help you to establish the situation and to find out how you can help the customer effectively.

Build rapport with your customer

The following points offer guidance on how to build rapport:

- When you are in a face-to-face situation, give the customer a warm greeting and a genuine smile.
- Listen carefully to what the customer is saying in order to understand their point of view. Active listening is one of the simplest secrets of customer service. Remember to be aware of what the customer is communicating non-verbally as well as hearing what they are saying verbally. Look out for signs (including body language) that they are displeased.
- Use positive communication. Even if you are handling customer service requests on the phone, a smile can come through in your voice. Make sure you are ready to be friendly.
- Show understanding and empathy. Customer service often involves emotions so it is important to ensure that you are always courteous and respectful. Never allow your own emotions to take over or influence the situation.
- Say thank you after every transaction. Customers appreciate good manners and they will remember your polite attitude. Regardless of the type of organisation you work for, this will reflect well on you and will reinforce customers' views of the organisation.

Link

Module 8: Communication (verbal and non-verbal communication)

Module 9: Interpersonal skills (active listening)

- Let customers know if you are unable to help them with their enquiry. Explain the reasons clearly and let them know where they might be able to get the product or service they are looking for. They will remember how helpful you were, even if you couldn't sell them what they needed.

How to respond appropriately using information from the customer

Once you have the information you need from the customer, it is important that you act appropriately:

- Confirm what the customer needs, as this will help to manage their expectations.
- Once you know what your customer is looking for, explain the products or services that may be suitable for them.
- Ask customers for feedback so that you can disregard any products you know will not be useful for them.
- Remember to demonstrate enthusiasm to help and a 'will-do attitude', but never promise what you know you cannot deliver.

Link 

Module 5: Products and service knowledge (explaining the features and benefits of your organisation's products and services)

Activity

Responding to the customer

Scenario

A new customer comes into your computing and IT store. She is browsing the personal computers and laptops on display. She approaches you to ask about the difference between the features of two different laptops.

1. What would you do first when the customer approached you?
2. List the questions you need to ask the customer in order to understand their computing requirements.
3. What would you do to make sure you had the right answers?

Summary 

- You should now know what is needed in order to deliver a customer-focused experience.
- It is important that you understand the customer's needs and expectations before you try to help them.
- To do this, you must build a rapport with them and ask questions to gather all the facts.

Understanding how to build trust with a customer

For a customer to trust an organisation they must believe that what the organisation is offering is worth purchasing. Disreputable organisations may try to gain sales without considering or caring about their customers' wellbeing. This will result in a breakdown of trust which, in turn, will mean that other, more honest, organisations have to work harder to maintain their reputation and their customers' trust.

Why is building customer trust important?

Some businesses don't consider trust to be critical to their long-term growth. However, trust is essential to a strong customer relationship. Building trust increases customer loyalty, sales and the likelihood that customers will recommend your organisation to other people. Loyal customers require less time and financial commitment for marketing new products and services than new customers. A recommendation from a friend or colleague is far more powerful than your promise because customer views are **impartial**, whereas your promise is **biased**.

There are several levels of trust, as shown in Figure 1.

First level of trust: technical competence and know-how
Clients and customers are looking for someone whose level of competence inspires trust.

↓

Second level of trust: ethical conduct and character
Your company's reputation is top of the list, and your honesty and integrity must be first class.

↓

Third level of trust: your interpersonal skills and relationship
You must ensure that your clients and customers believe that if they tell you something about themselves, their business or any sensitive information, you will handle it with the utmost respect and confidentiality.

↓

Fourth level of trust: being transparent and open in your business relationship
A lack of **transparency** will make you much more vulnerable to damaging any business relationship.

Figure 1: The four levels of trust

Key terms

Impartial – fair and without bias.

Biased – when someone or something is unfairly prejudiced in a certain direction.

Transparency – being open and honest about your activities.

How can you start to build trust with a customer?

There is no short-cut for instantly gaining a customer's trust: trust is something you have to earn over time. As shown in Figure 2, trust is one of the many benefits of a satisfied customer. If you can meet your customers' needs, you will start to build their trust.

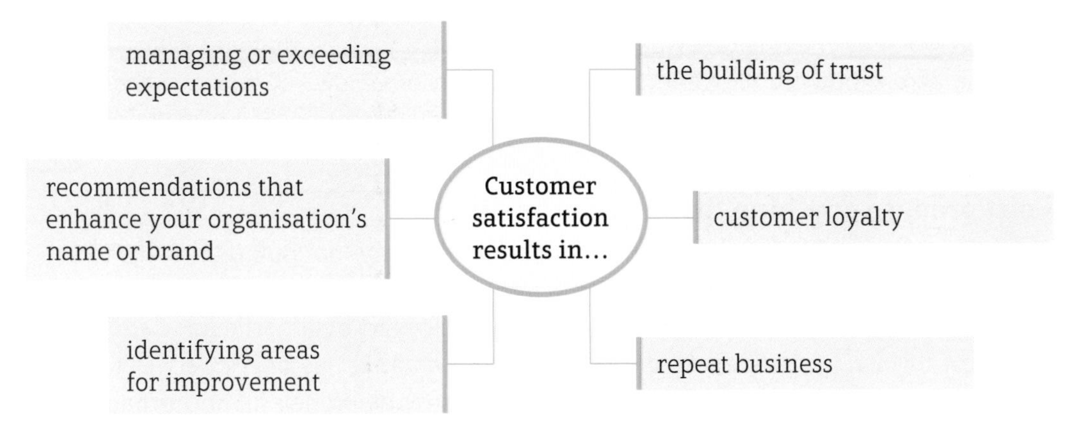

Figure 2: A satisfied customer will help your organisation in many ways

Consistently provide an exceptional customer experience

Exceptional customer experience makes customers want to come back. This includes every point of contact the customer has with your business, for example via the website, over the phone and during in-person visits. You need to make decisions based on your customer's needs and to display a positive personality in every communication. Treat each new face-to-face, phone or email encounter with a consistently positive attitude, whether it is your first encounter of the day or your last. Treat every customer equally and give everyone the same amount of time and effort.

Link 

Module 2: Meeting regulations and legislation (The Equality Act, 2010)

Listen

An essential part of customer service delivery is listening to what the customer is saying. Make sure you understand what they want and their expectations. This shows that you respect their views and that you are taking note of their needs.

Deliver quality and timeliness

Never deliver anything less than what you promised the customer. Delivering quality service every time, on time, shows customers that they can rely on your business in the long term. Once they believe that, you will have gained their trust.

Invite customers to review you

Encourage existing customers to leave feedback about their experience online. This shows customers that you trust them and positive reviews will help to improve your image for any new customers researching your organisation online.

Respond to negative reviews

If you deal with your customers online, take time to respond to every review, even the negative ones. Publishing a response to negative reviews shows new customers that you are capable of handling yourself well when things don't go as expected. It also shows that you care about your customers' experiences and are willing to make it right and exceed their expectations.

Summary 

You should now:

- appreciate the importance of building trust with your customers
- understand the behaviours you must demonstrate in order to build customer trust, such as listening and maintaining a positive attitude.

Dealing with customer conflict and challenge

When working in a customer-based environment, it is likely that you will come across both conflict and challenging behaviour. How you manage these situations effectively is key to your success as a customer service practitioner.

Key term 

Proactive – taking control and moving a situation forward before an issue occurs rather than dealing with a situation after it has happened.

Don't promise anything that you can't deliver

Some customer service practitioners find it difficult to say 'no' but, ultimately, this does not help you, the customer or your organisation. If you tell a customer that a product with specific features or benefits will be delivered by a particular date, when you know this isn't possible, you will destroy any trust that has developed. Deliver on your promises, exceed the customer's expectations by being helpful and **proactive**, and admit your faults if or when they occur to avoid customer conflict developing.

Be honest and transparent

Customers will appreciate if you are upfront and honest about your product knowledge or level of experience, even if it means you cannot help them. If you mislead them and any misinformation is later discovered, you will have damaged their trust in you and your organisation.

Activities

Difficult requests

A customer wants you to ship a product in a colour that you've never even heard of. How would you deal with this issue?

Trust

What would make you trust an organisation with your business?

How good is your customer service?

Ask a colleague to phone your organisation with an enquiry about a product or service. Record your conversation with them, or put the call on loud speaker. After the call, ask them what they thought of the service they received and how they felt about their customer experience.

Key term 

Goods warranty – a written statement issued by your organisation or a product's manufacturer that promises to repair or replace an item within a certain period of time after purchase.

Conflict

Customer conflicts can develop in various ways. They may be due to:

- mistakes made by the organisation
- customer error, such as ordering an incorrect item
- legal limitations relating to the sale of items, such as the expiry of a guarantee or **goods warranty**.

Challenge

Challenging behaviour can arise in a number of different situations, as shown in Figure 3.

Figure 3: You may have to handle different kinds of challenging behaviour while at work

As a customer service practitioner, it is your job to maintain a calm attitude and be patient in challenging situations:

- First, show the customer that you understand their point of view and that you care.
- Understand that you cannot control anyone else's behaviour. Although you only have control over your own actions, you can influence how customers respond to you to some degree.
- Keep your self-control. Never argue with customers when they are angry, displeased or complaining. If you become angry, sarcastic, irritated, bored or dismissive, you will have lost control of the situation. Remember, you can lose a good customer by showing these emotions.
- Stay calm, apologise sincerely for any problems and ask, 'What can I do to help?'
- Listen and let the customer speak. The customer wants to be heard, acknowledged and understood.
- Ask open questions to get an understanding of the situation.
- Use body language or listening noises to communicate that you're listening.
- Maintain eye contact (without staring).
- Use appropriate communication skills and techniques for dealing with conflict. Remember that your language and facial expressions communicate your attitude and that people often respond more to *how* you say something than what you say.
- Take ownership of the problem and try to solve it (or ask someone else who you know can solve it). Even if solving the customer's problem isn't part of your job description, never say this to the customer. Try to gain as much information as you can about the situation and then tell the customer how you can help. Be proactive and focus on finding a mutual solution to the issue. If possible, make a digital record of what has been agreed and email it to the customer afterwards.
- Don't blame the customer or your organisation. When explaining your store's policy or trying to clarify what went wrong, use either an indirect approach such as 'There are a few questions I need to ask before I can offer you a refund', or 'I' statements such as 'I need some additional information before I can offer you a refund'.

Link 

Module 8: Communication (verbal and non-verbal communication)

Module 9: Interpersonal skills (body language)

Module 10: Influencing skills

- Don't acknowledge that you or your organisation is to blame. You may not always know all of the facts and an admission may result in the customer taking legal action.
- Don't make promises you cannot keep. You must always follow your organisation's procedures. If you are unsure about anything, seek help from a more knowledgeable colleague, or someone with more authority.

Using signposting to meet customers' needs and manage expectations

Signposting is when you pass a problem that is outside your area of responsibility or authority to a senior colleague. This may happen if:

- you do not have the level of knowledge or expertise to resolve the problem
- it is a technical issue and you need to pass it to the appropriate department
- it involves, for example, a large refund to a customer and you are unable to authorise that sum of money.

Before passing on the problem, be sure to let the customer know what you are doing, then follow your organisation's procedures for escalating the issue. This could be via a face-to-face meeting with your manager or supervisor, or by emailing another department. Make sure that you have provided all the information your colleagues will need so that they can avoid going back to the customer. Keep the customer informed.

Figure 4 details how and when to signpost a problem.

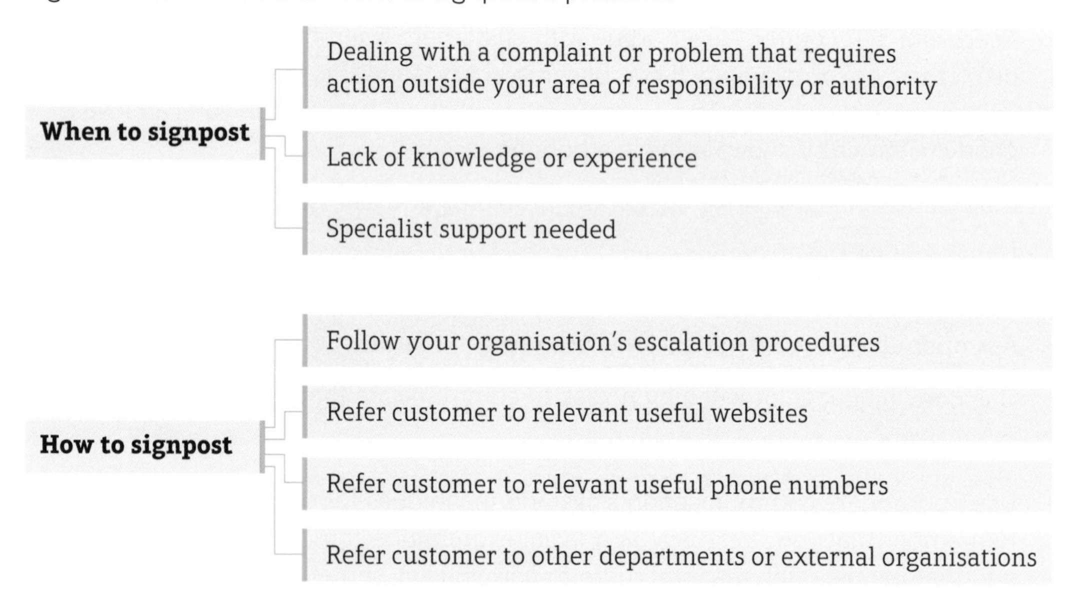

Figure 4: It is important to understand how and when to signpost a problem with a customer

Maintaining communication with the customer during service recovery

Service recovery is a response to a previous service failure on the part of your organisation. One of the major reasons for customer conflict and challenge is a breakdown in service.

Think about a time when a company failed to turn up on an agreed date to repair something at your home, or when a recently purchased piece of equipment broke down. You probably felt annoyed, especially if you had to take time off work to let them in. It is also likely that your trust in the company was damaged. The Professional working feature on this page explores how you can enhance customer experience and satisfaction in a service recovery situation.

Professional working

- The first step in the service recovery process is listening to the customer and understanding their perspective and priorities.
- Make sure that you and the customer mutually agree any actions you will take (and confirm in writing).
- Be sure to inform the customer of any changes or delays in providing products or services.
- Agree and maintain communication with your customer. If you promise to call or email, make sure that you do.
- Keep the customer informed of progress on any complaint or dispute in the service recovery process.
- With each step taken, make sure that the customer is happy with the progress.
- Keep accurate records of the process to guarantee a successful outcome for both the customer and your organisation.

Summary

- You should now understand the issues involved when dealing with conflict and challenge from both your own perspective and that of the customer.
- It is important to remember that an unhappy customer will not return and will let others know about their experience.
- Deal with conflicts effectively and resolve issues promptly.

Equality: treating all customers fairly and as individuals

To provide a personalised customer service experience, it is important that you treat each customer fairly and as an individual.

Link 

Module 2: Meeting regulations and legislation (The Equality Act, 2010)

Your organisation will have mission statements and equality policies. It is important that you read these documents and follow the guidance they contain. Remember the phrase: 'Treat others as you would like to be treated yourself'. The mind map in Figure 5 lists a number of ways in which you can ensure you are treating your customers fairly.

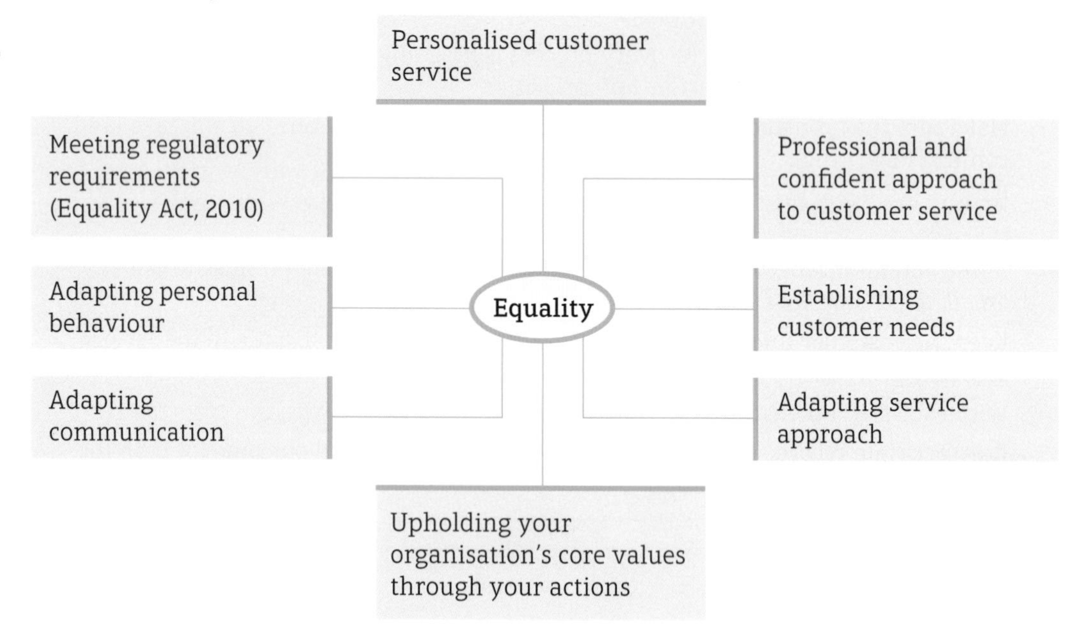

Figure 5: Equality involves treating people fairly to ensure that all customers' needs are met

Some products are visually designed to appeal to a stereotypical idea of a particular gender, but it is important when providing customer service that you highlight all options available to all customers.

Activities

Unequal treatment

Scenario

A woman enters a large hardware store and asks the customer service assistant for information about purchasing a power tool. Later that day, a man enters the same hardware store to buy a power tool and approaches the same assistant for advice. The department manager noticed that the customer service assistant did not treat the two customers equally.

1. Give one example of how the customer service assistant in the scenario might show a disregard of the importance of equality.
2. Give one example of how the customer service assistant could have demonstrated the correct behaviour.
3. How might the assistant demonstrate gender bias either consciously or unconsciously?

Perks and discounts

A customer asks for a perk or discount that you can't honour for other customers. How would you deal with this situation?

Refund requests

A customer demands a refund for a subscription they've already enjoyed for seven months. How would you deal with this situation?

Summary 

- When dealing with customers, it is important that you treat people equally.
- You should not demonstrate any personal bias regarding gender, disability, race, age or social status when making decisions about customer requests.
- All organisations should have equality procedures for you to follow at work and it is important that you read and understand them.

The following activities will help you strengthen the skills you have learned in this module about the customer experience.

Activities

Reflective account

Think about how you build trust with your customers. Use the reflective cycle to demonstrate how you would take steps to gain customers' trust.

Have you ever seen a colleague deal with an angry customer? Reflect on the outcome and how it might have been different depending on their behaviour.

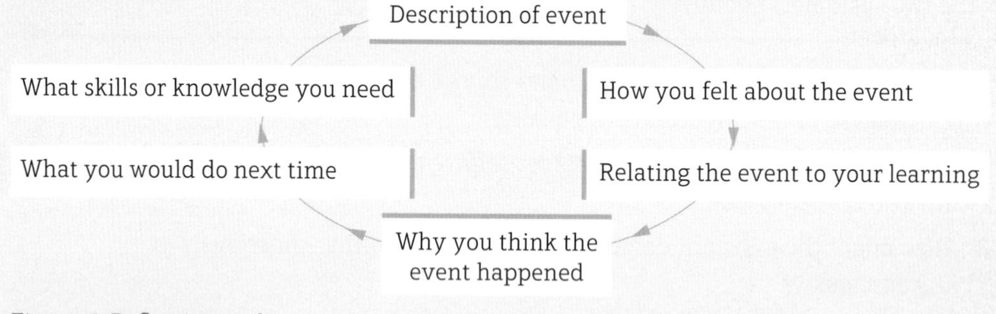

Figure 6: Reflective cycle

EPA preparation

A veterinary nurse has been caring for a dog who has undergone an operation. The next day, when she returns to work, she finds that the dog has passed away.

Research the Elisabeth Kübler-Ross Cycle of Grief to see how this might apply to a customer service situation of this kind.

Behaviours

Explain an appropriate way you would deal with an angry customer in the context of your own workplace.

8

Communication

What is communication?

Good quality customer care depends on good quality communication. Communicating well can be challenging but also rewarding.

In this module, you will explore different and creative ways to overcome barriers to communication, so that you can help your customers and share information effectively. You will learn about:

- verbal and non-verbal communication
- face-to-face and non-facing communication
- opening communication in order to assess customers' needs and expectations
- 'right first time'.

Using verbal and non-verbal communication skills

Effective communication is at the heart of any successful business. An organisation's success relies on clear, concise communication delivered with confidence. As a customer service practitioner, you will be expected to adapt your communication in each new situation you encounter. Your tone, behaviour, verbal language and body language should be tailored to different customers and their individual needs, while ensuring that you treat each customer equally.

Verbal communication

Verbal communication is the use of appropriate language to deliver your message effectively. The words you use can help provide a positive message by reassuring customers about your intentions, for example 'I understand' or 'I will make sure that...'. Avoid using technical phrases or jargon unless you are sure that the customer knows their meaning.

Non-verbal communication

Non-verbal communication is interaction without speaking. It is the non-language elements of communication and includes body language such as touching, the pitch and tone of your voice, the volume of your speaking voice, your facial expressions, eye contact and your posture (how you stand or sit), as well as your clothing and the personal distance between two or more people. It may also include mirroring behaviour, which is when one person imitates the expression, gesture or attitude of the person they are talking to, sometimes without realising that they are doing so. As a customer service practitioner, you can use mirroring behaviour positively, for example by using appropriate facial expressions to show empathy for a customer's situation. Negative mirroring, by contrast, could include pointing a finger or scowling.

Using body language to maintain or enhance customer experience

As a customer service practitioner, you are '**front of house**' staff. This means that you are among the first people seen or encountered by the public. You should therefore use positive body language in order to provide the right service. Your facial expression is very important in creating an immediate bond with customers. You should be welcoming and friendly, as this will make you appear approachable. Inappropriate expressions include slouching, frowning, daydreaming or looking disinterested. Negative attitudes such as these could damage your chance of forming good relationships with customers and, as a result, damage your organisation's reputation. Think carefully about how you should appear to your customers in your opening communication (see Figure 1).

Key term 

Front of house – customer service practitioners who meet and greet customers, or who are the first point of contact for customers who send emails or call with a query.

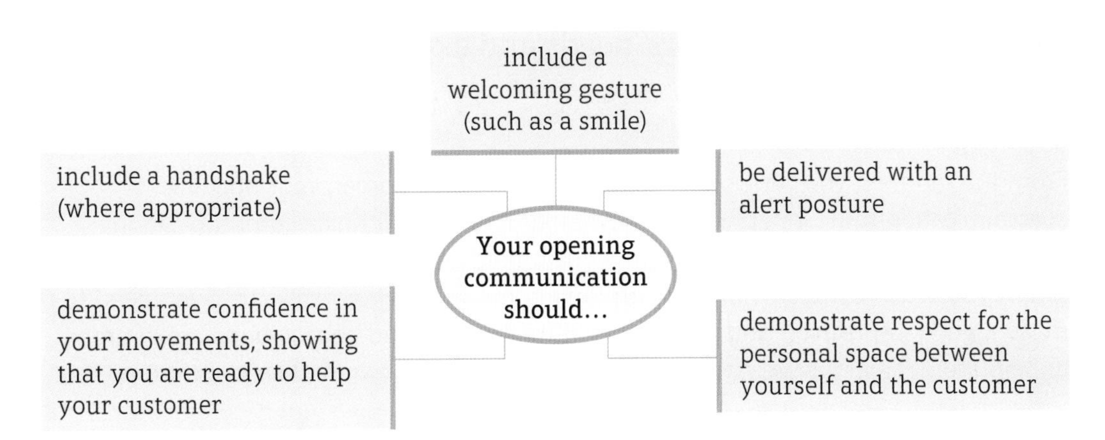

Figure 1: It is important to make a good first impression on your customers

Adapting your tone and behaviour

Your tone of voice is as important as the language you use when dealing with a customer. You should:

- sound enthusiastic and friendly
- make sure you use the correct words and phrases to avoid any offence
- maintain a suitable pitch in your voice: don't raise your voice even if the customer seems angry
- speak slowly and calmly, leaving appropriate pauses to help the customer understand your view
- make sure there is no room for doubt or misunderstanding – your message should be straightforward and clear
- have confidence in the message you are delivering
- listen to what the customer is saying and do not interrupt.

Professional working 

The UK is a multicultural society and has both residents and visitors from all over the world. It is important to be aware of cultural differences, particularly in body language, and to adapt your behaviour and body language accordingly.

For example, it is unacceptable in Middle Eastern countries to touch females who are not members of your family. In other cultures, the left hand is used for bodily hygiene functions so you should avoid shaking hands or using personal items with your left hand.

Eye contact is encouraged in some societies but in some Asian countries it is considered to demonstrate a lack of respect.

Link 

Module 9: Interpersonal skills (body language and cultural differences)

Confirming your customers' needs and expectations and those of your organisation

Opening communication

From the moment you have your first contact with a customer, your opening communication must be appropriate. Whether it is a face-to-face communication (when you are physically present with a customer) or a non-facing communication (when you are in contact with them on the phone, or via an email/letter), you need to make a good impression and find out what their needs and expectations are in order to help them. This may be dependent on who they are or where they come from.

Link 

Module 9: Interpersonal skills (open and closed questions; active listening skills)

In your opening communication you should:

- be friendly and caring
- be attentive and interested in the customer to demonstrate a positive attitude
- listen carefully to understand what the customer requires or needs
- ask open questions such as 'What are you looking for today?' and closed questions such as 'Is this suitable?'
- answer questions in a warm and friendly way at all times, but especially when customers are upset or have a complaint
- show a willingness to help with any problem the customer may have (they do not want to hear 'No' or 'Sorry, it's not my job')
- give clear, correct information on products or services requested by the customer to meet their requirements
- check your understanding of the customer's answers by summarising what they have said – this will reinforce your mutual goals and will give the customer the opportunity to correct any misunderstandings.

Link 

Module 6: Knowing your customers (customer needs and expectations)

Module 10: Influencing skills (customer needs and expectations)

Professional working 

Remember the acronym GUEST:

G – **G**reet your customer

U – **U**nderstand your customer's needs

E – **E**xplain a product or service's features and benefits to identify the most appropriate option for your customer

S – **S**uggest additional items that may be of interest to the customer in order to further promote your organisation

T – **T**hank the customer and check that they are satisfied.

Using summarising language to check your understanding

Closing communication

When bringing a conversation with a customer to an end, it is important to make sure you summarise what has been discussed in order to reinforce their expectations. Allow the customer to explain everything to you and then ask them if there is anything else they would like to add. Encourage them to put forward their point of view, without interruption; this creates a good rapport and shows that you care about them.

- Repeat or **paraphrase** what has been said. It is important that you take notes, especially if it is a complicated issue.
- Make sure that you have all of the relevant information required to take the enquiry forward. Let your customer know whether you need to ask your line manager for guidance.
- Discuss, and then agree, the next steps with the customer so that they know there is a plan in place to deal with their enquiry.
- Follow up with the customer at a later stage to ensure that a satisfactory outcome has been reached.

Key term 

Paraphrase – to reword something (either written or spoken) in order to make it clearer.

Communication and your organisation's brand

Using communication skills effectively is an important part of promoting your organisation's brand:

- **It helps to create a relationship –** by delivering a consistent service, you help to strengthen the connection between brands and customers. Without consistency, customers might begin to lose trust in the brand.
- **It reduces customer confusion –** a clear identity and message is crucial in establishing a long-standing relationship with a customer.
- **It helps to maintain expectations –** with good communication, organisations can ensure that they deliver on internal and external communications right down to the smallest details. If they know what to expect from a brand, customers may be willing to pay more for services.

With verbal communication, it is your voice that helps bring your organisation's personality to life. If you give customers the correct verbal and written information, you will increase their awareness of your brand. The 'voice' of the organisation impacts the way your customers feel about you. Remember to:

- use correct spellings in any written communication – use the spellchecker on your computer
- use straightforward language, be mindful of your tone and avoid jargon.

Professional working 

Use correct, appropriate and clear communication skills (both written and verbal) to reflect your organisation's brand.

Summary 

You have learned that:

- communication is varied and can take many forms – verbal, non-verbal or a combination of both
- how you communicate in your formal writing and in your facial expressions and gestures can positively or negatively influence your relationship with your customer
- as a customer service practitioner, you should always be aware of your tone and behaviour so that it enhances the customer's experience.

'Right first time'

As a customer service practitioner you should understand how to speak to customers correctly, and the importance of getting the right information to customers as soon as possible and managing their expectations. This is known as being 'right first time' (see Figure 2). You need to conduct yourself in a professional manner while following your organisation's procedures and guidelines.

Link

Module 2: Meeting regulations and legislation (The Equality Act, 2010)

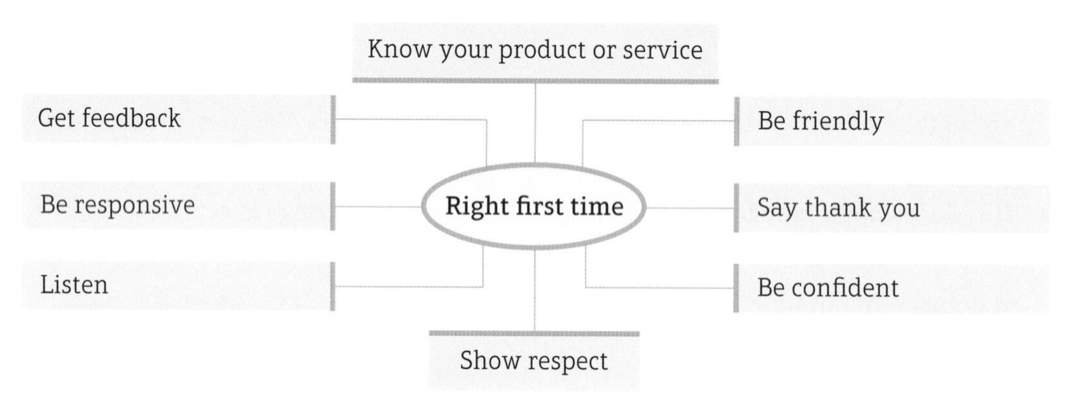

Figure 2: Customer service practitioners need to be 'right first time'

It is important that you take ownership of the situation from your first contact with the customer. Work hard to resolve their issue and then take responsibility for fulfilling any promise you make to them. Use your verbal and non-verbal communication skills to show you are open and genuine in your approach, even if there is disagreement between you. Be constructive, even if you disagree with a customer's point of view. If you cannot provide a solution to a customer's problem immediately, gain as much information as you can and then refer the issue to your line manager to find out what you can offer the customer or how you can help them.

Remember that you shouldn't pass a problem on without first gathering information about the issue and trying to help. Customers will not want to repeat the issue to a second person: make sure you paraphrase the problem to your manager so they know what to expect.

The three scenarios below ask you to consider how you would use your communication skills to establish what your customer needs and how to manage their expectations. Remember to:

- present yourself professionally (in both manner and personal appearance)
- follow the industry standard requirements for your organisation
- use positive language and body language
- read the customer's signs and signals to make a decision on how to adapt your service approach
- treat all customers equally.

Activity

Getting things right

1. List some practical ways you can ensure that you get things right in your opening communication (both written and in person).
2. How would you deal with an angry customer who demands to see the manager?

Activity

Lacking information on a call

Scenario

You take a call from a customer who is enquiring about an order that they placed. You realise you do not have enough knowledge about the product they are talking about and you are unsure of the information you need to gain from the caller.

- What should you do in this situation?

Link 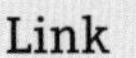 

Module 9: Interpersonal skills (building rapport)

Customers may ask for help to resolve an issue or they may want to find out more about what you are selling.

Respond quickly to all enquiries, even if only to say you are looking into the issue. If necessary, ask a more knowledgeable colleague about a product and explain to the customer that you will be back in touch. Some response is always better than no response. This will ensure that the customer doesn't feel ignored.

Professional working 

Use your communication skills to ensure you:

- make a good first impression on your customer
- build a rapport with your customer using positive body language: avoid folding your arms and maintain an appropriate posture
- listen carefully in order to understand your customer's requirements
- take ownership of the interaction with your customer by asking 'How may I help you?'
- maintain contact with your customers to let them know what is happening, especially if you are dealing with a problem over the phone and the customer has been 'on hold'.

Summary 

- In your role as a customer service practitioner, it is vital to ensure that you make a positive first impression on your customers from the initial moment of contact (being right first time).
- You are your organisation's representative and, as such, have a responsibility to promote your organisation's image or brand using effective communication skills.

The following activities will help you strengthen the skills you have learned and used in this module about communication.

Activities

Reflective account

In an average working week, you will deal with customers with many different requirements. Create a table using the headers shown in Table 1 and make a record of the most important or difficult requirements you dealt with in one week at work. Use this as evidence for your apprentice showcase.

Customer requirement	How did you deal with it?

Table 1: Summary of customer requirements

EPA preparation

As you have seen in this module, communication is an essential part of the customer service role. Research information and images, using books or the internet, to create a 'Pie chart of communication'. Think about the approximate percentage of the pie that should be allocated to:

1. verbal communication
2. tone of voice
3. body language.

For example, do you think most communication occurs via body language or through the language you use when you speak? Perhaps you think there should be slices of the pie allocated to other forms of communication.

Your percentages do not need to be precise and you may not agree with other people, but be prepared to explain why you have suggested your percentages.

Behaviours

As part of a listening exercise, gather together a group of your colleagues and tell them a short story. Afterwards, ask each person to repeat back what you said, in as much detail as they can remember. This activity will demonstrate the importance of good listening skills and help you to develop one of the essential communication behaviours.

9

Interpersonal skills

What are interpersonal skills?

In a customer service setting, you will be required to interact with customers using different forms of communication. In so doing, you will develop your interpersonal skills by exchanging information, feelings and meaning with both customers and colleagues.

In this module, you will learn:

- about different interpersonal skills and how to use them to recognise customers' needs and expectations in order to deliver professional customer service
- how to build and maintain a rapport with your customers
- about the importance of teamwork
- how to seek, accept and act on feedback from colleagues and customers.

Interpersonal communication

Communication is a two-way process. It involves at least two people who are listening and responding to each other. There are different methods of communication. You could be face-to-face with someone, or you could be sending an email or using the phone. All of these methods require two, or more, people. One person will begin by talking or writing – they are the sender of the message. The other person will receive the message and respond by talking, smiling, gesturing (for example by nodding) or writing.

Elements of interpersonal communication

Interpersonal communication includes the following elements:

- **Sender:** the person who sends a message using verbal or non-verbal methods.
- **Receiver:** the person who listens to the sender, reads the sender's message or observes the sender's gestures and tone of voice.
- **Message:** verbal or non-verbal communication.
- **Noise:** this can either be physical noise (for example a dog barking or a train passing by) that prevents the receiver from hearing the sender, or anything that prevents the sender and/or receiver from understanding one another, such as the use of language that neither person will understand, a lack of attention, connectivity issues in online 'virtual' meetings, inappropriate body language or cultural differences.
- **Feedback:** this could be verbal language or body language and it indicates the sender or receiver's intention or reaction.
- **Context:** this might be the physical place in which an interaction is taking place (for example, a store or a meeting room), or the social context in which senders and receivers come together from different social or cultural backgrounds, bringing different expectations or attitudes.
- **Channel**: the method via which the message is being sent, for example a face-to-face conversation, an email or letter, or the telephone.

Figure 1 shows the process by which a message (either verbal or non-verbal) is sent from the sender to the receiver via a particular channel. It shows the message being received and understood, and the feedback that is returned to the sender (the response).

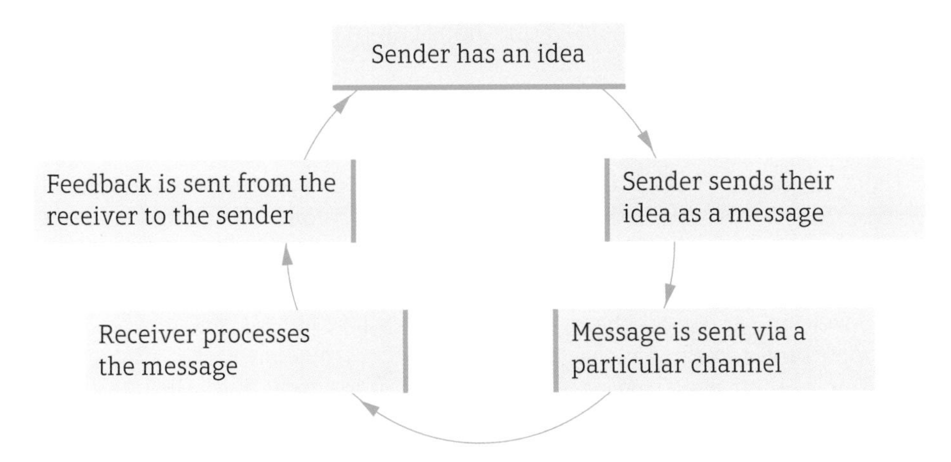

Figure 1: The communication process

Demonstrating effective interpersonal skills to engage your customer

As a customer service practitioner, it is important to start a conversation with a customer positively and to build a relationship with them (a **rapport**) as quickly as possible. You can do this by:

- being clear – think before you speak and have a purpose and clarity in what you are saying; don't ramble
- being confident – demonstrate to your customer that you are sure of what you are saying; if necessary, give an example to make the customer feel that they can trust the information you are providing
- thinking about the pitch and tone of your voice – the customer will lose interest if you maintain the same volume in your voice, if you speak too fast or too slow, or if you come across as impatient or disinterested.

Key term 

Rapport – a relationship between two or more people in which each person understands the other and everyone communicates well.

Using open and closed questions

When dealing with a customer you need to begin the conversation by using questioning techniques in order to gather information and check understanding. You can use open or closed questions to gain information from the customer:

- Open questions require a full answer, not simply a 'Yes' or 'No' response. These questions may start with 'What', 'Why', 'When', 'How', 'Describe' and so on.
- Closed questions can be answered with a single word or phrase, such as 'Yes', 'No', 'Absolutely not!' or 'Yes, indeed'.

Figure 2 shows what a difference open questions can make when gathering information.

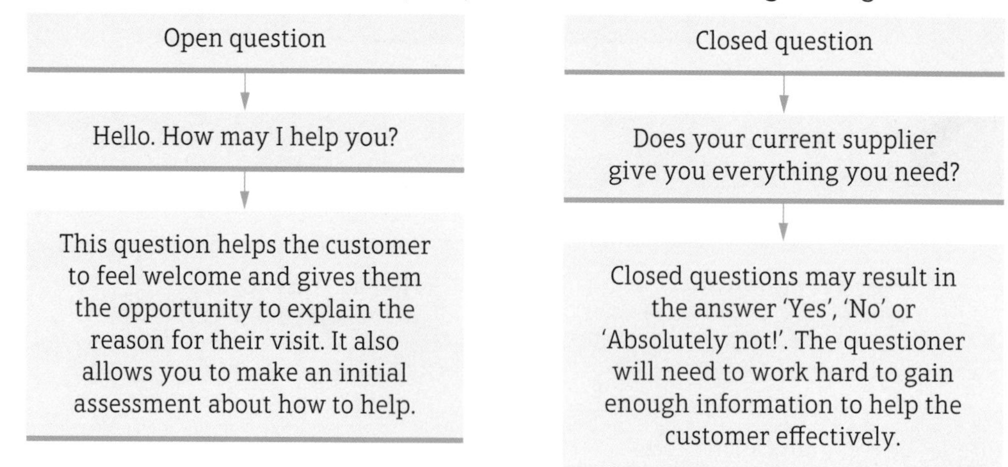

Figure 2: It may be easier to use open questions when gathering information from customers

Link 

Module 10: Influencing skills (questioning skills)

Activities

Role play

Ask a colleague to help you to role play a scenario in which one of you is a customer and the other is the customer service assistant. Start by taking the role of the assistant. Ask the customer (a) a mixture of open and closed questions, then (b) closed questions only, then finally (c) open questions only. Swap roles so that your colleague takes the role of the customer service assistant.

1. How did you feel in each role?
2. What did you notice about the different sets of questions (a), (b) and (c)?
3. Which sets of questions gave you more information?

Closed and open-ended questions

1. Visit a retail store (preferably one where they don't know you) and try to remember every question the salesperson asks you. Note how many closed questions they ask. List open-ended alternatives that would have helped them make the sale.
2. Think about your last interaction with a customer and the language you used. How many closed questions could you have swapped for open ones?

Professional working 

Questioning techniques are an important part of your interpersonal skills. When starting conversations with customers, balance out the different types of questions you ask: approximately three closed questions to one open question. Closed questions start the conversation and summarise progress or understanding. Open questions get the customer thinking and encourage them to give you useful information that you can then use to process their enquiry.

Using active listening skills effectively when communicating

Listening is arguably the most important interpersonal skill. Many people take listening for granted as it is something that just happens.

Effective listening can help to form strong relationships with others both inside and outside of the home – socially, in education and in the workplace. Effective listening is therefore an important skill that you will need to develop in your role as a customer service practitioner.

Consider the following points when you interact with customers:

- Be attentive – make sure the customer is aware that you are listening to what they are saying.
- Try not to interrupt – you might miss a vital piece of information needed to help the customer.
- If it is a complicated issue such as a complaint, ask the customer if you can take notes – that way, you have a record of exactly what is needed.
- Make sure that you repeat back any information – this demonstrates your understanding and provides the customer with the chance to correct any information you may have misunderstood.
- Show empathy – empathetic listening means understanding the feelings and emotions of the speaker, putting yourself in the speaker's position and sharing their thoughts. Empathy is not the same as sympathy, it involves more than being compassionate or feeling sorry for somebody else. It involves having an understanding of another person's point of view.
- Use appropriate body language.

Figure 3 details some of the ways in which you can ensure you listen with your whole body.

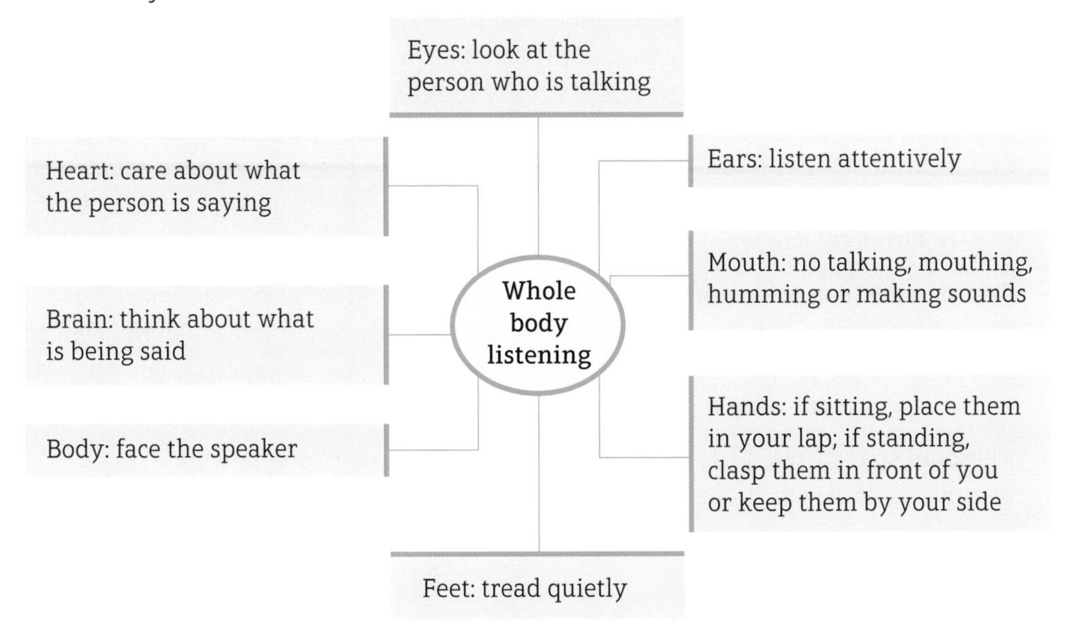

Figure 3: When a customer is talking to you, listen with more than just your ears

Using body language in customer interactions

Body language is a type of non-verbal communication that demonstrates feelings, emotions, attitudes and thoughts through body movements. These movements might include gestures, your posture (how you stand or sit), eye contact, head movements or hand movements. Whether you are dealing with customers or giving a presentation at work, you must be aware of how to use body language effectively. Here are some guidelines:

- **Eye contact:** Always maintain eye contact with your customer but avoid fixing your gaze or staring at one person for more than a few seconds as this can be disconcerting. By contrast, too much eye movement can suggest a lack of confidence or exaggeration of the truth.
- **Handshaking:** Your handshake should be firm, not loose. However, avoid an 'iron' handshake (an extremely strong grip), as the customer might think that you are trying to dominate the situation.
- **Crossing your arms:** It is best to avoid crossing your arms as this could imply that you are not open to new ideas or opinions.
- **Open and closed postures:** Customers may be put off by a closed posture, for example someone seated with their arms folded, legs crossed and body at a slight angle to the person speaking. By contrast, an open posture, such as someone sitting upright, in a relaxed position facing the speaker, with their arms apart, makes you appear approachable. Be careful not to sit too far back in your chair – this might imply a lack of interest or rejection.
- **Gestures:** Gestures are a type of non-verbal communication in which someone uses a part of their body with or without verbal communication. Gestures include facial expressions, nods (a sign of approval in most cultures), head bobbing or head shaking.
- **Facial expressions:** Smiling is an important part of positive body language and can help you to appear warm and approachable. Your face is a reflection of what you feel. More often than not, it is easy to recognise if a person is happy, sad, anxious, irritated or excited. However, in a professional scenario, it is very important that you control your facial expressions. For example, if you smiled when someone was complaining about the customer service in your company, they might think you were not taking their complaint seriously.
- **Appropriate tone and volume:** Non-verbal communication also includes voice tone, pitch, speed, volume and any pauses you include to convey meaning. For example, if you were giving a presentation and looking for a response, you should pause. If you don't want a response, you could talk faster with minimal pauses.
- **Personal space:** Avoid sitting or standing too close to customers when communicating with them. If you are too close to someone (especially their face), you could be seen as aggressive or inappropriate.

Activity

Developing a rapport

Scenario

You work as a customer service assistant in the children's section of a library. One day, you are tidying up the shelves when a customer approaches you. She mentions how much her daughter liked the book that you have just put back and starts describing the parts her daughter enjoyed the most.

List the actions you would take to:

- show the customer that you are interested in what she is saying
- develop a rapport with her.

Dealing with a language barrier

Scenario

You work in a bank as a customer service practitioner. You have set up a meeting with a customer, Mr Rahman, who is looking for a loan to open a business. Mr Rahman struggles to communicate well in English. You are trying to explain to him that the bank turned down his request for a loan because his business plan will not generate enough income. You both grow increasingly frustrated as you try to discuss the issues.

How could you overcome the language barrier and the growing frustration between you and Mr Rahman in order to communicate this negative decision effectively?

Smiling will help to show that you are warm and approachable. However, you should consider that smiling is not always appropriate if, for example, a customer is making a complaint.

The impact of cultural differences on non-verbal communication

Non-verbal communication can vary considerably depending on your culture and country of origin. If you work with people across the world or deal regularly with non-native English speakers, you need to understand how to communicate effectively with them.

Examples of cultural differences include the following:

- Eye contact – the length of time it is appropriate to hold someone's gaze can vary. For example, in Asian cultures, avoiding eye contact is seen as a sign of respect whereas in North and South America eye contact implies equality.
- Touch – in Western cultures, a firm handshake is considered appropriate when greeting a stranger or business professional. Touching children on the head is also appropriate. However, in Asia, this is considered highly inappropriate, as the head is seen as a sacred part of the body. In the Middle East, people use their left hands for bodily hygiene so using that hand to accept a gift or shake hands is considered extremely rude. Cultures also differ when it comes to physical contact between men and women.
- Gestures and signs – the same gesture or sign may have different meanings depending on where and with whom you use it. For example, people in the United States use the 'OK' sign to mean that something is good. However, in Japan, the same sign means 'money'. Other nationalities (including Argentinians, Belgians, French and Portuguese) use this sign to mean 'zero' or 'nothing' whereas some Eastern European countries consider it to be offensive.

The American 'OK' sign has different meanings in many countries

Recognising customer needs and building and maintaining a rapport

Once you recognise and respond to a customer's needs and expectations, you can use your interpersonal skills to develop and maintain a rapport with them.

The benefits of having a good rapport with customers are that they will:

- like and trust you
- communicate more openly with you
- feel confident in your abilities and product knowledge
- respond well to you closing a sale.

Use positive and appropriate verbal and non-verbal communication when responding to customers.

- Listen carefully.
- Ask questions to understand what the customer needs, then use your knowledge of your organisation's products, and their features and benefits, to satisfy the customer's requirements.
- Show empathy to demonstrate that you understand the customer's situation, especially if they are making a complaint.
- Use your body language to demonsrate an appropriate and caring manner. Use open gestures and show genuine concern.
- Treat disagreements carefully and professionally. Do not argue with the customer, try to give clear reasons when dealing with disputes and, if necessary, refer them to your line manager.

Link 

Module 6: Knowing your customers (recognising and responding to customer needs and expectations; managing expectations in a professional and timely manner)

Module 8: Communication (body language; GUEST acronym)

Module 10: Influencing skills (customer needs and expectations)

Summary 

You have learned about the different elements of interpersonal communication and how you can use them, together with questioning skills, listening skills and body language to:

- engage your customers effectively
- build rapport
- enhance the customer service experience.

Working together as a team to help customers efficiently

Teamwork is an important part of a business. You need to work well with your colleagues, sharing the workload when necessary and trying your best at all times. Good teamwork means that people will try to cooperate, using their individual skills and demonstrating professional behaviour. As part of a team, you need to be able to communicate effectively and work together to deliver your organisation's service standards and to achieve your agreed objectives and deadlines. This often means sharing information, especially when dealing with customer problems or complaints.

Interpersonal skills for effective teamwork

As a member of a customer service team, you need to use effective personal behaviours, communicate consistently and demonstrate cooperation when working with others.

- Being a good team member means being able to communicate your ideas to your colleagues. This will help you to offer the best possible service to your customers.
- You must be able to convey information over the phone, via email and in person. You want to ensure your tone is professional, polite and friendly. Both verbal and non-verbal communication is important when working with a group.
- Colleagues (both in your immediate team and other departments or branches) will be more open to communicating with you if you show respect for them and their ideas and values. Remember that you will be working with people from different cultures and with different beliefs. Simple actions, such as using a person's name, making eye contact, and actively listening when they speak, will make people feel appreciated.
- You must be willing to learn from other, more experienced, people in your team. Always follow your team leader's instructions.
- Communicate regularly with your colleagues to make sure you can help your customers, suppliers and your whole team (including managers, supervisors and colleagues in other departments). This may include giving colleagues constructive feedback, and accepting and acting on feedback from others.
- Responsibility and accountability are important in problem solving. Accept responsibility when helping to solve customers' problems, for example by saying that you are going to do something and then following through on your promise. Meet any deadlines you have been set. This builds trust between you, your colleagues and your customers, and demonstrates your reliability.

Sharing personal learning

It is good working practice to share your personal learning with others, so present any ideas or recommendations for improvements you have to your team.

- If you have an idea or an example of how you provided good customer service, share these case studies with your team so they can benefit everyone. This could include feedback from a written or digital communication, an example of how you spoke to a customer or supplier in a way that resulted in a positive outcome, or an example of how you followed organisational procedures in the correct manner.
- Don't be afraid to seek assistance or advice from others; if you cannot deal with a problem, pass the case to a senior colleague or manager.
- Team meetings or one-to-one meetings are ideal places to communicate your ideas. If you rely on digital communication, use email to pass on any useful information that may help others to provide better service.
- Be aware of opportunities to share ideas for improvement in reports, blogs or training sessions. You can then discuss any lessons learned. What went well? Which areas could be improved? How could you ensure that, if you found yourself in a similar situation, the result would be more positive?

Activity

Reflecting on past experiences

Scenario

You are preparing to interview for a higher position in your company. At your interview, you will meet with a three-person panel. They will probably ask you questions such as 'Give examples of your teamwork'. This question asks you to reflect on your past experiences in order to show how you would act in your new position.

1. Describe your work experience.
2. Describe your team, and your job role within it.
3. Give an example of a goal that was set for your team and how you contributed to its outcome.

Summary 

- The way in which you conduct yourself will have an impact on both your team and your organisation.
- Negative behaviour demonstrates poor teamwork and can be damaging to your organisation's image and brand. Such behaviour might include not 'pulling your weight', so that other members of the team have to do your share of the workload, being unreliable or untrustworthy, or being impolite.
- Positive behaviour, such as resolving customers' problems, sharing ideas and meeting deadlines, will not only improve your confidence, but enhance your organisation's image and profitability.

Act on, and seek, feedback from others

It is important to get feedback from your team and manager. This is important in developing your personal skills, confidence and motivation. If you use the feedback you receive, you can take responsibility for maintaining your own service skills and knowledge.

Whether you are giving or receiving feedback, it needs to be:

- **specific and actionable** – suggestions should be based on observed behaviour (what you notice) or fact; do not make any assumptions based on what you know of someone's character
- **constructive and purposeful –** feedback should be led by curiosity (by asking questions and listening) and motivated by a desire to help; even if a task or project has gone well and objectives have been met, you should seek feedback
- **timely and in an appropriate setting –** feedback should be provided when the person receiving it is in the right frame of mind to do so; do not wait too long to deliver feedback.

You should seek feedback during longer tasks and projects as well as after they have finished. If you are only given feedback after a project is complete, it means that there is no chance to amend your work as you go along. This may be seen as unfair and unhelpful. Figure 4 provides more information on feedback.

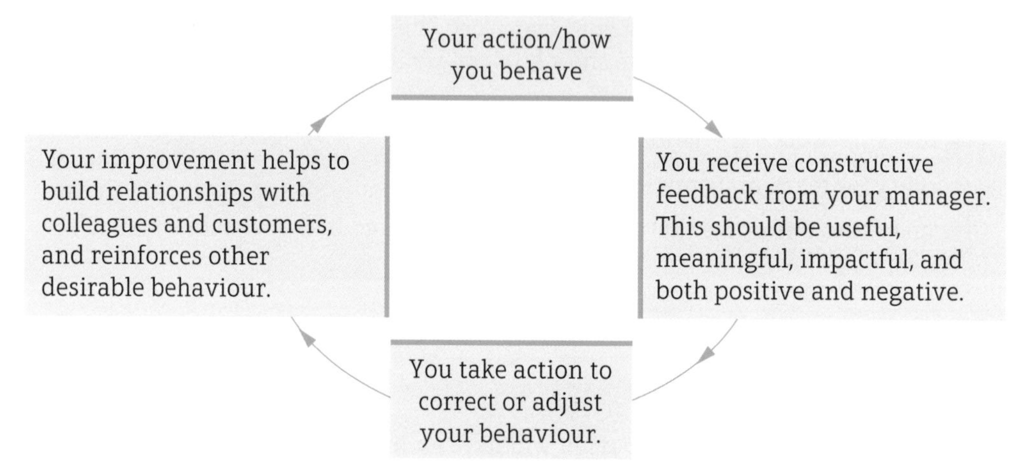

Figure 4: Feedback enables you to continually improve your customer service

Feedback should be delivered during formal performance appraisals, in which you will be given information on how to develop your goals and increase your future skills. However, you can also ask your manager to provide feedback on an informal basis, as you carry out your daily work, as this can be both constructive and useful.

Listen to any feedback you receive and ask questions to make sure you understand what is being said. You should not take it as criticism; it is necessary to help you develop. Be positive when receiving feedback and ask for advice to help you improve.

Activity

Positive feedback

Scenario

Your manager says to you: 'Great job today. I noticed how you're applying the things we've been talking about in our one-to-one meetings. Your tone of voice was more authoritative, you used non-technical language that the customer could relate to, and your message was clearer and more focused. When you compare your performance today to what I observed last month, you've come a long way.'

1. How would you react to this positive feedback?
2. What questions could you ask to get a clearer understanding of the feedback?
3. Can you think of any other ways to show that you are responding positively?

Professional working

Use any feedback you receive as an opportunity to take responsibility for maintaining and developing your personal customer service skills and knowledge.

For example, after a presentation your manager takes you aside and says: 'I know you put a lot of work into today's presentation, not only with all the data you gathered from other departments, but also the hours you put in over the weekend. I appreciate the extraordinary effort. It shows your commitment and will go a long way towards helping the team feel prepared when they talk to clients. Next time, let's figure out how we can save you some prep time.'

Think about what your manager is suggesting. How could you use this feedback to develop your skills?

Summary

- You need feedback in order to develop your personal skills.
- It is important that you seek out and receive feedback in both formal and informal situations.
- Remember to take feedback positively and ask questions to check your understanding.
- Your manager should be experienced in the different ways of delivering feedback.

The following activities will help you strengthen the skills you have learned in this module about interpersonal skills.

Activities

Reflective account

Enter the phrase 'body language' in an internet search engine. Note down any interesting findings in a notebook, to be used as part of your apprentice showcase.

EPA preparation

Analyse your own communication skills. What are your strengths and weaknesses? Think about your colleagues' communication skills. Make some notes on yourself and your colleagues. Use your notes to create a presentation on communication skills. Do not name your colleagues in your presentation.

Behaviours

When you have the opportunity to observe some interpersonal communication, make a note of the behaviours used – both verbal and non-verbal.

1. Who are the people that are communicating?
2. What are they trying to say?
3. Is there background 'noise' that could affect the communication?
4. How is feedback given and how is it received?

By observing others, you can continue to develop your own interpersonal communication skills.

10
Influencing skills

Delivering informed choices

You can influence internal or external customers by providing clear explanations and offering options. It is important to learn how to do this so you can meet their immediate needs and also benefit your organisation by suggesting additional products or services.

In this module you will learn about key factors to ensure you can:

- identify customer needs and deliver excellent customer service
- offer a product or service that meets both existing and potential customer needs
- explain the benefits of a product or service to the customer
- handle any customer objections in a professional manner, and build and maintain rapport (a good relationship).

Customer needs and expectations

It is easier to do business with organisations that are recognised for the quality of their products or services and have a good reputation. It is important for organisations to maintain this good reputation by continuing to meet (and exceed) customer needs and expectations. If they do not meet customer needs and expectations, they could damage their reputation.

Key terms

Negotiating – being able to discuss and reach a mutually satisfactory agreement.

Influencing – being able to affect or change how someone or something develops, behaves or thinks (a combination of persuading and negotiating).

Persuading – being able to convince others to take appropriate action(s).

Assertiveness – clear and direct communication – being assertive allows you to state what you want and to say 'no' firmly without causing offence.

Link

Module 8: Communication

Module 9: Interpersonal skills

Influencing your customers

Have you ever changed your rota days in order to get a Saturday or evening duty covered so that you can go out? Did you suggest to your colleague that you would take on a task you knew they didn't like in exchange for covering your shift? If so, this was a form of **negotiation**. You **influenced** and **persuaded** your colleague to give you what you wanted.

In your job role, you can use your influencing skills in the same way by discussing possible solutions with customers and reaching a satisfactory conclusion.

There is no right way, nor is there only one way, to influence people. You will need to consider many factors when influencing your customers.

If you can influence people effectively and ensure that everyone feels comfortable with the outcome, you will make your job easier. Both you and your customer will get what you want out of the situation. Good influencing skills require a combination of:

- effective interpersonal skills (being able to use listening and questioning skills well)
- good communication skills (being able to use verbal and non-verbal skills well)
- the ability to present options (giving the customer informed choices)
- **assertiveness** techniques.

Understanding your customers

An individual customer's needs and expectations depend on their characteristics and lifestyle.

- If you meet a customer's needs, you will have a positive impact on customer satisfaction and return sales.
- If you meet a customer's expectations of a product or brand, it is likely you will keep the customer and build a long-term relationship with them.

Activity

Wants, needs and expectations

Scenario

Charlie is 26 and single. He has a good full-time job in IT but the office is 25 miles from where he lives. He has saved up some money to buy a car as he is fed up with waiting on cold platforms for trains that are often delayed, and walking from the station to his office in the rain. Image is important to Charlie. He feels that the way he dresses and the car he drives is important, but he also needs the car to be reliable and cheap to run. He has seen three cars: a 14-year-old sports car, a two-year-old luxury saloon and a six-month-old economy hatchback.

In Table 1, column 1, state what you think are Charlie's wants, needs and expectations. Give reasons for your answers. Once you have identified these, decide which car you think Charlie should buy and why.

Charlie's...	What have you identified and why?	Which car would you recommend and why?
wants		
needs		
expectations		

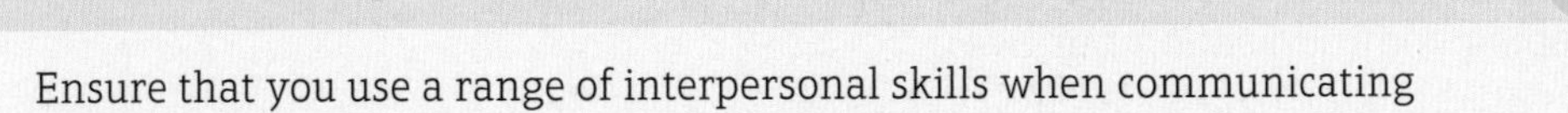

Table 1: Charlie's wants, needs and expectations

Link 

Module 3: Your role and responsibility (equality and diversity)

Link 

Module 6: Knowing your customers

Professional working 

- Ensure that you use a range of interpersonal skills when communicating with customers.
- Ensure that you use appropriate verbal and non-verbal communication.
- Use communication behaviours that clearly establish what individual customers require. Manage their expectations to provide a personalised customer service experience.

Summary

- Treat each customer as an individual.
- Summarise conversations to clarify your understanding and that of your customer.
- Keep up to date with products and services, and be able to explain their benefits.
- Recognise the difference between needs and expectations.
- Practise being assertive.

Offering products or services to customers

As the market and technology changes, so will your organisation's products or services. It is important to offer appropriate products and services to your customers.

Always listen to your customer to ensure that you identify the most appropriate product or service to offer them based on their needs. You should be able to give clear descriptions of the benefits of any product or service, and explain how they meet your customer's needs. For example, you may need to help customers complete application forms and explain why it is important for them to give detailed information.

You may be asked to provide a solution for your customer by demonstrating, for example, how to access a new application on a mobile phone. Or you may need to explain a service that your organisation provides. Ensure that you give positive verbal or non-verbal communication in a professional way.

When using verbal communication, listen carefully and respond to the customer's questions, or summarise what you believe they said.

It is important to use open questions and read the customer's body language. Open questions will get more detailed information from customers, not single-word answers.

Link 

Module 8: Communication

Tips for good communication include:

- effective listening
- knowing when to be quiet
- keeping communication positive
- **empathising** and apologising where appropriate
- summarise the information you are given
- influencing and achieving an outcome that is agreeable to all.

Key term 

Empathising – being able to share and understand others' feelings – you may, for example, have experienced the same scenario or situation.

Influencing and negotiating

In order to influence your customers, you need to provide clear explanations to help them make choices that benefit them and your organisation. They should be happy with the options you offer them.

- Be realistic by offering a delivery date you can meet.
- Know how much discount you are allowed to offer – can you offer a second product half price?
- Know the limits of your own authority – do you need to ask your manager or supervisor for help?

The customer journey: capturing feedback

The cycle in Figure 1 shows each stage of the customer journey. After you complete a transaction or deliver a service, it is important to gather feedback. You can use this feedback to improve a service or decide whether to continue to offer a product.

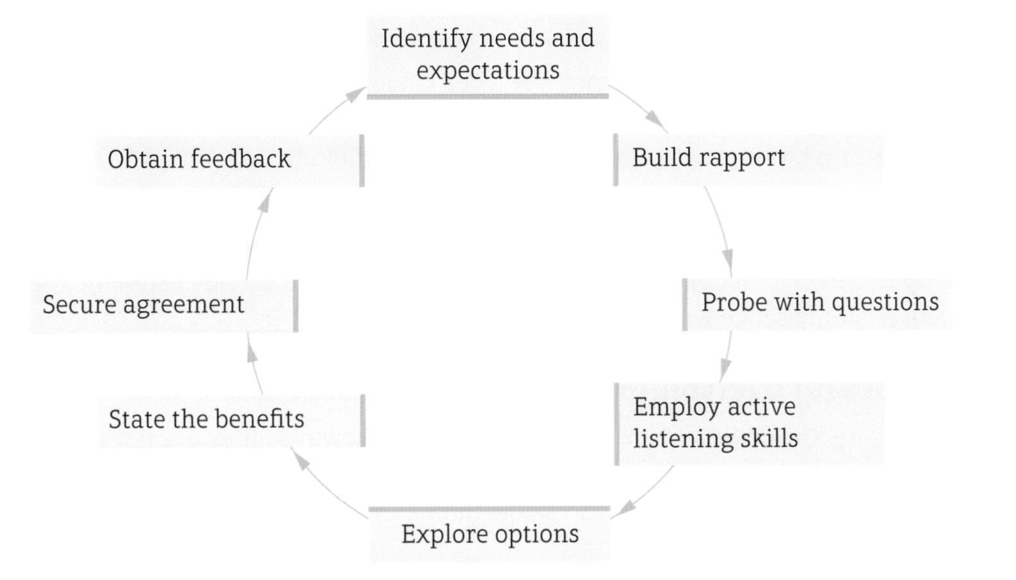

Figure 1: Use the stages of a customer journey to improve your customer service

Link

Module 6: Knowing your customers

Activity

The customer journey

1. Figure 1 shows a customer's journey. Relate this cycle to your own department or role. (You could use a similar format to Figure 1 or one of your own.)
2. What techniques did you use to keep your customers happy? How did you balance the needs of your organisation? Where did you need further support?

Summary

- Understanding the customer journey will help you move from their first enquiry to meeting their needs in a logical sequence. Can you present your own customer journey?
- Make sure you know your organisation's policies and procedures for handling customers. They may have a code of practice for you to follow.
- All organisations need feedback from their customers. Make sure you know how your organisation gathers feedback and how it acts on it.
- Often, what a customer *wants* is not what they really *need*. You can use effective customer service practices to identify their needs and realistic expectations. You can then aim to deliver on those expectations.

Handling customer objections to build and maintain rapport

Wherever you work, it is important that your customers do not go elsewhere for similar products and services. To help with customer retention (keeping customers) you should deal with complaints immediately.

Link 

Module 6: Knowing your customers

Link 

Module 7: Customer experience (handling complaints)

As you gain experience, you may be able to spot situations in which things could go wrong by observing customer behaviour and body language, and by listening to the language customers use when they are unhappy.

Techniques for overcoming barriers

Complaints are inevitable in a customer service role. However, they are not the end of the line. You do still have a chance to influence that customer. Make sure you know the limits of your role so that you can tell your customer when you may need to pass their query on to a manager.

Remember the following points:

- Understand why the customer is objecting.
- Remain positive and professional at all times.
- Take the time to identify why they have made a complaint.
- Try to move the conversation forward in a way that benefits everyone by negotiating a solution.
- Consider whether the customer fully understands your product or service, and reinforce the benefits of their features.
- Consider whether customers have specific concerns that they have not raised – perhaps from something someone else has said or something they have read.
- Consider whether customers have other reasons for being annoyed that they have not told you.
- Consider customers' perceptions of your product or service.
- Have you listened carefully and summarised your understanding of the customer's real needs?

Activity

External customers

Scenario

Matteo owns a beauty salon. He received an angry complaint from a customer. She said that one of Matteo's staff had been rude and prevented her from using a tanning booth. She felt that, as a regular customer, she should be able to use the equipment without an appointment. The booth had been free but Matteo's staff member had explained that another customer was due shortly. They said she wouldn't be able to use the booth immediately but that she could make an appointment for another time. The customer became angry and shouted at the staff on duty. She then contacted Matteo to demand compensation.

1. What steps should Matteo take?
2. Why should he take these steps?
3. Should Matteo do anything to ensure that this does not happen again?

Professional working: skills and behaviours

You need to be able to demonstrate that you can stay calm in challenging situations. Maintain contact with the customer and show that you understand their point of view. You should take ownership of the situation from first contact and follow up on your promises.

You will observe both good and bad communication within the workplace. Apply the same concepts to any negotiating you need to do.

Activity

Internal customers

Scenario

You hear Samir and Keila discussing the new tidy desk policy. Keila says she has been in trouble with her manager. She says it is impossible for her to keep her desk tidy because she has to store things on her desk for Samir and there is no room for her own work.

Samir says that because Keila is new and does different work, she does not need as much space as he does. He says that he has always kept some of his things on the desk next to where he sits. Keila stands up and shouts that this is unfair and nobody told her that this is the usual practice.

Refer to the key tips for good communication on page 124 to answer the following questions:

1. Did Samir and Keila use active listening skills?
2. Did they ask the right questions?
3. Did they look at each other's body language?
4. Did they identify any related needs?

Link

Module 6: Knowing your customers (equality and diversity)

Module 11: Personal organisation

Key term

Concession – offering an allowance, special rate or gift to compensate for a faulty product or poor service.

Summary

Customers will feel reassured that you are helpful and knowledgeable if you show confidence when you offer a product or service. You should:

- make sure you keep up to date with any changes in your products or services
- know who to ask if you have a query
- know how and when to ask advice from other departments
- know how and when to take a complaint to a senior member of staff
- respect your customer and offer an apology where appropriate, or a **concession** or alternative offer.

The following activities will help you to strengthen the skills you have learned in this module about influencing customers.

Activities

Reflective account

1. Think about occasions when you influenced and/or negotiated with customers to ensure that their needs were met. Add these details to your reflective log.
2. Using work completed in this and other modules, give two examples of how you worked with others, solved customer objections and managed your time to meet customer needs.
    a. What did you learn from this?
    b. Would you do anything differently if the same situation arose?

EPA preparation

On page 125 you drew a diagram to show your customer journey.

1. Prepare a presentation about a situation in which a customer challenged you or complained.
2. At what stage of the journey did this happen? What behaviour did your customer display?

Behaviours

1. Complete Table 2 to give three examples of products or services you have offered.
2. In each case, say whether you had to offer alternative options, what benefits/features you explained and whether you met the customer's needs.

Product or service originally offered	**What options did you offer?**	**What benefits or features did you explain?**	**Did you meet their needs? If not, why not?**
1.			
2.			
3.			

Table 2: Meeting customer needs

3. Give an example of a time when you recognised that the customer's body language did not match what they were saying. How did you manage this situation?

11
Personal organisation

Organising yourself effectively

At work, it is essential that you organise your time, energy and resources efficiently, so that you can achieve your day-to-day and long-term tasks. Self-discipline and good organisational skills are crucial to success in any profession.

In this module, you will learn the importance of:

- organising yourself and setting your own deadlines
- adjusting your way of working to meet deadlines based on changing priorities
- continually monitoring your own progress
- taking ownership of maintaining your knowledge and skills
- presenting yourself according to an appropriate dress code and using professional language.

Agree goals and deadlines for completing tasks

A key part of personal organisation is being able to prioritise your short- and long-term tasks on a daily basis. Knowing the objectives and timeframes for those tasks will make it easier to organise your time efficiently.

Why do you need to meet work standards and deadlines?

It is important to meet your organisation's work standards and deadlines – failure to do this could affect whether your company meets its **objectives**. Every organisation must meet its customers' needs and expectations in order to maintain its brand image and profitability. Working as part of a team, you must demonstrate your reliability by meeting your deadlines, in order to build the trust of your customers and colleagues. Achieving deadlines will also help to build your confidence and make it less likely that you will need to be continually supervised by your managers or mentors.

Key term

Objective – something that is aimed for; a goal.

How does your work contribute to the team effort?

All members of a team are required to achieve goals and meet deadlines. Even if you work on your own, it is highly likely that your role will be part of a wider team, who will expect you to deliver results and achieve tasks by a particular time.

Advantages of teamwork

Some of the advantages of working as a team are as follows:

- Teamwork increases collaboration and promotes an idea-sharing culture. This often results in increased productivity and creativity.
- Two or more people are always better than one when solving problems as they will bring different perspectives and knowledge to a situation.
- Teamwork teaches you how to develop your interpersonal skills through effective communication and information sharing.
- Working with others to coordinate schedules, meet deadlines, share the workload and make decisions will strengthen your working relationships.

Link

Module 6: Knowing your customers (customer needs and expectations)
Module 7: Customer experience (building trust)
Module 9: Interpersonal skills (teamwork)

How can you agree your goals and deadlines?

You and your manager should meet to discuss what goals need to be set and how you will achieve them within the deadline. Agreeing realistic goals is a process. It starts with careful consideration of what your organisation requires of you, what you can achieve within your skillset and workload, and is followed by hard work and dedication.

These are the main rules when setting goals:

- **Motivation:** Goals should motivate you. You must make sure that they are important to you and that there is value in achieving them.

- **Set SMART goals:** For goals to be powerful, they should be designed to be SMART. There are many variations of what SMART stands for, but in this case, your goals should be designed as shown in Figure 1.

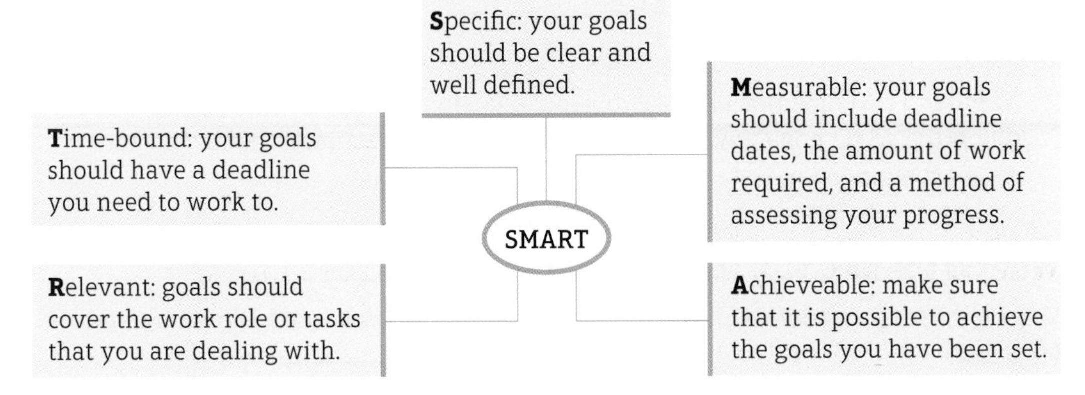

Figure 1: Successful goals are SMART goals

- **Goals should be in writing**: It must be clear what is to be achieved. Writing your goals down makes them real. Make sure that you ask your manager any questions that are relevant to the goals that have been set for you. If you don't understand what you need to do, ask for more explanation. If you don't, you risk wasting time trying to find out information that your manager could have clarified at the start.
- **Make an action plan:** While it is important to remain focused on the outcome, you must plan all of the steps that are needed along the way. By writing out the individual steps and then crossing off each one as you complete it, you will see that you are making progress towards your ultimate goal.
- **Stick to it:** Remember, goal setting is an on-going activity. Build in reminders to keep yourself on track and set regular time-slots in which to review your goals.

Activity

Choose one of your current workplace goals

To make sure that your goal is motivating, write down why it is valuable and important to you. Ask yourself, 'If I were to share my goal with others, what would I tell them to convince them it was worthwhile?' You can use this motivating value statement to help you if you start to doubt yourself or lose confidence in your ability to make the goal happen.

Summary

- You have learned that by setting goals and deadlines early you will not only help achieve your company's desired outcomes but also improve your personal organisation.
- Knowing that you and your team are working together to meet deadlines is motivational.
- Use your time efficiently by asking questions to clarify the way forward.

Prioritise and plan the completion of tasks to meet deadlines

Whether a deadline has been set by you, a customer or your manager, you are all 'on the same page' (working towards common objectives). Deadlines focus people's attention!

What is the best way to set deadlines?

You will need to consider a number of different things before agreeing on a deadline for a task:

- Agree the tasks that need to be completed and how long you will need to complete them.
- Look at your goals with your manager and/or your team, listen to what is discussed and make notes to help you understand what is required.
- Ask questions to make sure you are clear on what is needed to meet the deadlines set.
- Check the quality standards required to complete the tasks by their specific deadlines.

Set your deadlines within the same week or month, and keep to them. If a task is even more urgent, set your deadline for today. When you mark a task as urgent, treat your time as limited and you will keep yourself motivated and driven.

Tips for setting deadlines

Follow this guidance when setting deadlines:

- Write down your deadlines.
- Schedule each step on your calendar. This will prevent delays and missed deadlines.
- Plan your priorities. Prioritising means sorting out which task needs completing first, and ranking tasks in order of their importance or urgency. Give those tasks more of your attention, energy and time. It may be that ticking a particular task off your list first enables you to complete the rest of the tasks more easily.
- Think about how long a task is likely to take.
- Do the difficult parts of a task first.
- Identify personal 'roadblocks' that could prevent completion of tasks, such as lack of the correct equipment.
- Anticipate mistakes or delays so you can better plan for them.

Create an effective action plan

Use an action plan to prioritise your work. This is a document that lists the steps that must be taken in order to achieve a specific goal. Your action plan will help you to clarify which resources are required to reach the goal and to formulate a timeline for when specific tasks need to be completed. Use Figure 2 to help you to create your action plan.

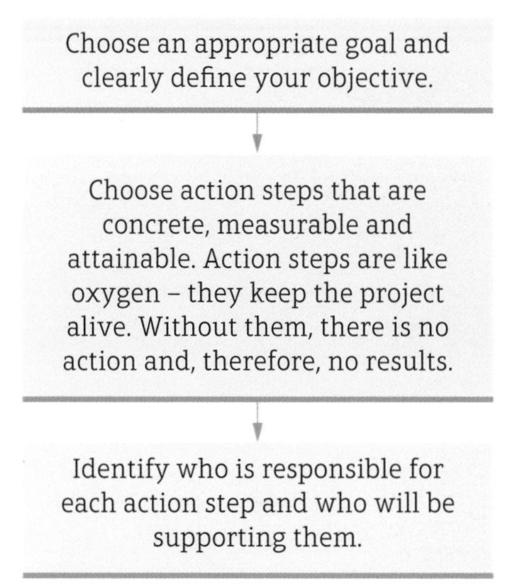

Figure 2: Flow chart to help to create an action plan

Activities

Preparing an action plan

A long-term goal is something you want to accomplish that may take a while to achieve, such as increasing your sales figures. Prepare an action plan that can help you to reach one of your long-term goals.

Creating a 'to-do' list

Note down your goals, then make a 'to-do' list of the tasks you must complete to achieve them. Post copies of this list in places where you will see it on a regular basis, such as your office walls, desk or computer monitor, to remind yourself every day of what it is you intend to do.

Use tools and techniques to monitor progress of tasks

There are tools and techniques (such as the action plans described above) that you can use to monitor your progress on tasks. Your organisation is also likely to have evaluation tools that will help, for example, to assess the average length of tasks, the time it takes to convert a lead and the average response time to answer a customer query. All of these methods will contribute to your overall understanding of your workload and deadlines. See Figure 3 for more guidance on monitoring your progress.

Link 

Module 4: Systems and resources (evaluation tools to monitor customer service levels)

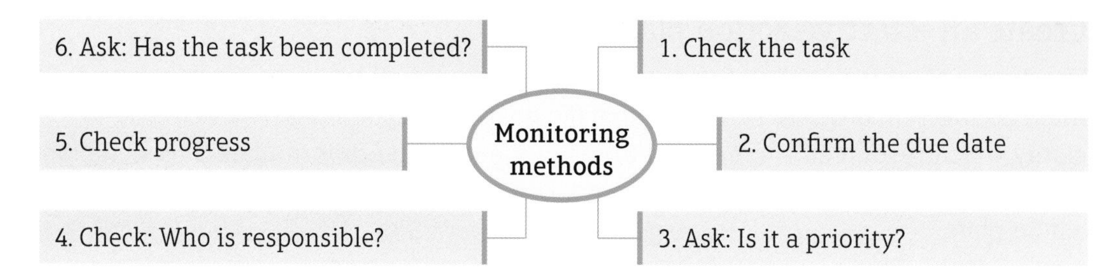

Figure 3: A step-by-step approach to monitoring your progress on tasks

Activity

Daily tasks

Scenario

You are working as a customer service practitioner in a veterinary clinic. You arrive at work one morning and find the following list of jobs for you to complete during the day:

- Check all the animals.
- Switch off phone diversion.
- Report any necessary information on the condition of the animals to the vet on duty.
- Sweep the floor of the reception area.
- Unlock the front door and change sign from CLOSED to OPEN.
- Place stock order.

You will need to:

- put these jobs in the order in which you feel you should complete them, explaining the reasons for your choice
- list any factors that might mean you'll have to change your planned order.

1. Which are the most important jobs on the list?
2. How may your jobs affect others working in the clinic?
3. Do any jobs need to be done by a set time in the day?
4. What factors may affect how or when you perform these jobs? How would you work around these?
5. What workplace policies must you remember while performing these jobs?
6. Could you perform any of these jobs better if you had help?
7. Who would you check with if you were unsure of which jobs to do first?

Make adjustments to priorities to meet agreed deadlines

It is important to check your progress on tasks and review your workload regularly to prioritise what needs to be done and to make sure you can meet your deadlines.

- Check the tasks that need completing and the time required to complete them. When setting your schedule, try to build in some agreed contingency time to allow for both planned and unplanned events, such as holidays or illness.
- Look at what may happen if the tasks are not completed on time, such as the effect on others in the team or on customers.
- Remember: work that requires a quick response (such as a customer who needs an answer to a problem by the end of the day) may take priority over important long-term projects that your manager expects you to work on. Don't be afraid to ask colleagues for help or advice on what the priority should be.
- Always have an alternative plan when dealing with a task. For example, if you know you have meetings that could affect your deadlines, look at whether you can allocate a particular time slot for tasks in progress.
- Work with your available time-management tools. These might include your calendar, schedule, reminder functions on your computer, diary, sticky notes on your desk or to-do lists.
- Avoid distractions or interruptions if you have a deadline to keep. This can sometimes be easier said than done!
- If you feel you cannot complete a task within the deadline set, it is important that you discuss it ahead of time with your manager or team and consider a new deadline. It is better to be upfront about the reasons for the delay rather than waiting until the deadline has passed. You need to avoid letting your customers or team down. There may also be implications for the delay further on in the process.
- Carry out regular checks on the accuracy and quality of your work and follow your organisation's guidance.

Managing your time and workload well will help you to achieve deadlines. On occasion, you may find that you need to reassess your priorities as work progresses. This may be due to a shift in your team's overall priorities, tasks that take longer than anticipated, or your manager deciding that a particular task is more important than the one you had originally prioritised, for example.

Summary

- A significant part of personal organisation is agreeing goals and deadlines with your manager and the rest of your team.
- Learn to prioritise the tasks that need to be completed first and to identify what can wait, then write this down in the form of an action plan.
- Demonstrate flexibility in your approach if priorities need to be adjusted.

Develop yourself

In order to make progress at work or in your personal life, you need to be actively developing your skills at all times. It is important that you take responsibility for developing your service knowledge and skills. Think about your strengths and weaknesses in your customer service job role. By understanding where you are strong and where you need assistance, you can improve both your professional and personal life.

Take ownership of keeping your service knowledge and skills up to date

There are many different ways for you to keep learning and developing your skills:

- Everyone makes mistakes at some point. The important thing is to learn from them to prevent the same errors re-occurring.
- Make sure your product knowledge is up to date. If there are new items available, for example, make sure you can answer any questions that customers might ask.
- Ask your manager or senior colleagues for feedback on your performance.
- Read magazine or internet articles about your business and about services specifically relating to your organisation's sector.

Improving your knowledge and skills will help your career progression, enhance your confidence and increase customer satisfaction. Some other advantages of keeping up to date are shown in Figure 4.

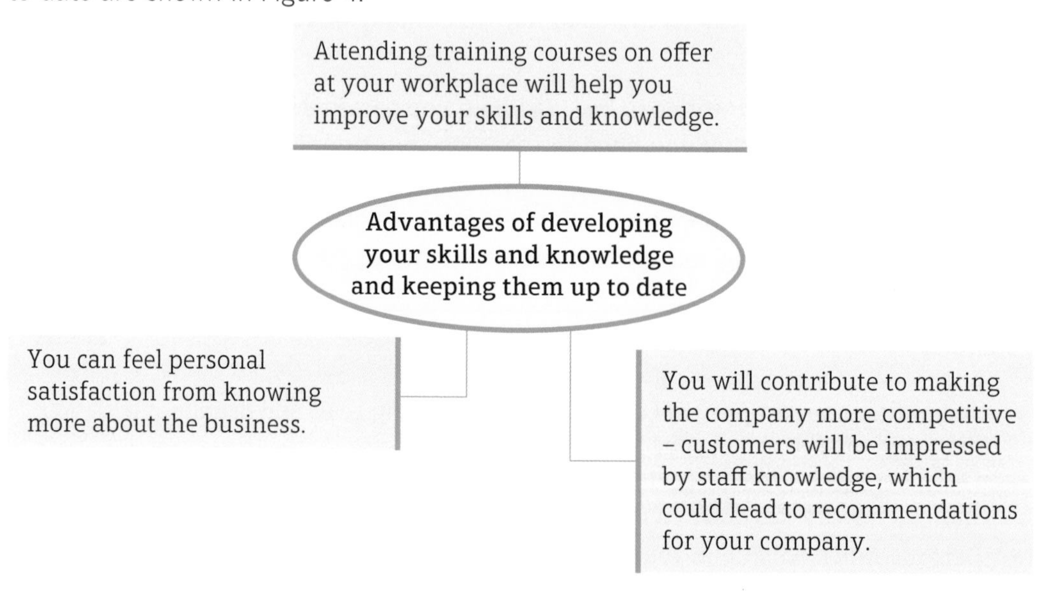

Figure 4: By continually developing your skills, you will benefit yourself and your company

Identifying gaps in your knowledge

In order to stay up to date, it is important to be aware of where there are gaps in your knowledge:

- Do a **skills audit**: compile a list of things you consider that you do well (your strengths) and a list of things that need to be improved (your weaknesses).
- To understand how well you are performing, ask your manager for constructive feedback, such as reviews and appraisals on your work. This could happen in a formal meeting or you could ask for their opinion after completing a particular task.

Key term 

Skills audit – a process in which you check and list your skills.

Activity

Developing yourself

1. The next time something goes wrong at work, make a note of what it was, what the circumstances were, who was involved and what you did at the time. It is best to do this soon after the event so you remember the context.
2. Reflect on what happened, then write down what you would do differently in order to improve the situation were it to happen again.
3. Were there any gaps in your knowledge or skills that prevented you from handling the situation correctly?
4. Suggest to your manager that you schedule a one-to-one to discuss the event and what you have learned from it. Ask for your manager's feedback on your solution.

Consider your personal goals and any development that would help achieve them

Personal goals help to push you forward in life. It is good to have an understanding of the significance of goal-setting and to apply this knowledge in your personal life.

When setting your personal goals, it is useful to include the following objectives:

- Gain relevant qualifications to improve your promotion opportunities or job prospects.
- Understand the experience that you may need – on-the-job training is important in developing product knowledge and gaining confidence in dealing with customers and colleagues.

Gaining information on personal development

When considering your personal development, it may help to:

- look at your job description – this will give you important information about the skills and knowledge you need
- look at the description of the type of person needed for a particular position – are they required to be enthusiastic and organised, for example?
- consider your team's objectives – this will help you identify your own strengths and weaknesses, and how these could affect the team's objectives (you may, for example, have excellent IT knowledge but feel less confident about sharing that knowledge effectively)
- get a clear idea of any training and development support available in your company.

Activity

Your PDP

Using your skills audit, draw up a personal development plan (PDP). The plan needs to include the following things:

1. Your goals or objectives.
2. Details of how to prioritise the most important goals and objectives.
3. A deadline – when planning, give yourself a realistic timeframe and remember the acronym SMART.
4. Your strengths – if you are not sure what you think your strengths are, ask your colleagues for feedback.
5. Any obstacles in the way of your development – what obstacles could block your progression?
6. New skills you need to develop – identify any skills you think you are lacking and consider how to gain this knowledge.
7. Actions you need to take in order to develop – write down 3–5 actions you need to take within the timeframe.
8. A list of who will support you in your plan, to include anyone who can help you to achieve your goals.
9. Details of how you will measure your progress – write down things that you are doing well and how to improve on things that aren't going so well.

Different types of learning and development activities

When considering how you can develop your knowledge and skills, think about a variety of methods such as:

- on-the-job training, or shadowing a senior/more experienced colleague to see how they work
- coaching or mentoring by an experienced member of your team (this may also help their progression to a more senior role)
- in-house training courses or job rotation opportunities
- external training courses, such as online courses run by suppliers to help increase your knowledge of their product(s) (this can be a win–win situation for you and the supplier)

When considering your PDP, think about your learning style. There are four main styles of learning:

- visual: you may like to see how things are done
- auditory: you may prefer to listen
- reading: you may prefer to read instructions
- kinaesthetic: you may prefer carrying out physical or practical activities when dealing with a task.

Reviewing the effectiveness of development plans

You should take part in regular reviews or one-to-one meetings with your manager to gain feedback on your performance and targets. Another useful way to make sure you develop both professionally and personally is 360-degree feedback (as shown in Figure 5). This involves getting feedback from colleagues, managers or supervisors, as well as completing a self-evaluation.

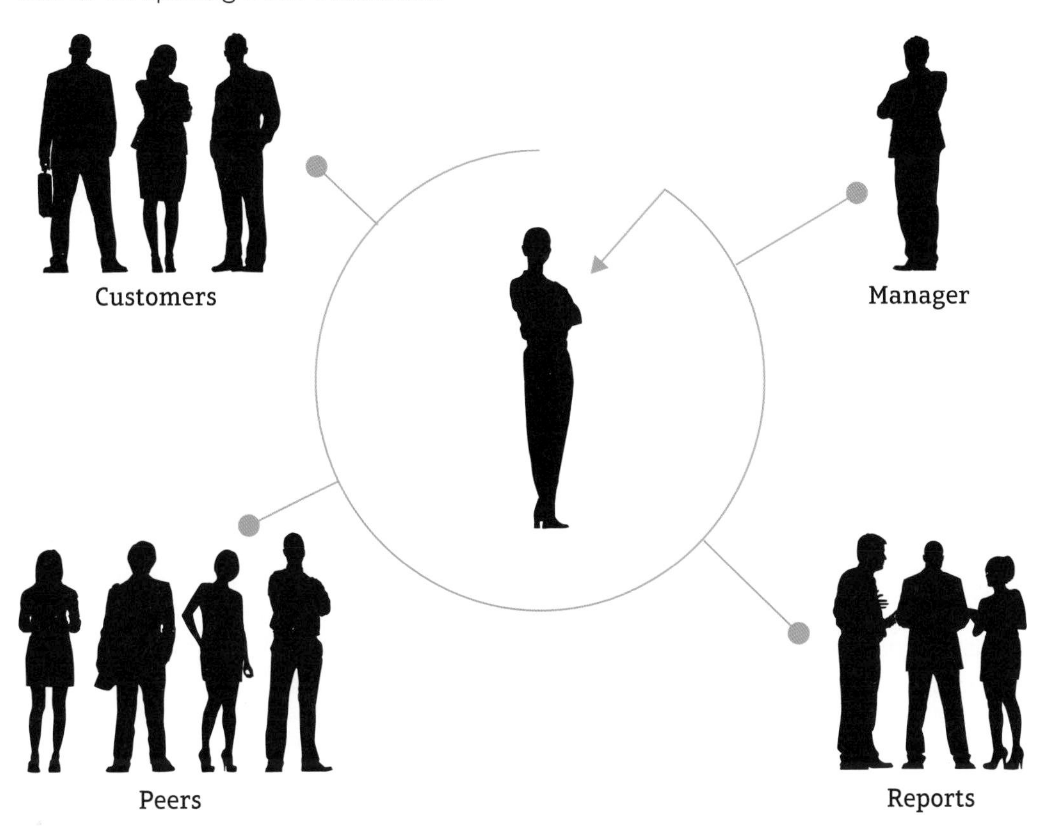

Figure 5: During 360-degree feedback, you will receive feedback from people you work alongside, as well as your managers

Activity

360-degree feedback

1. Practise giving and receiving 360-degree feedback with a colleague.
2. Work on any areas you feel you could improve and repeat the process later on in your course to see if you have done so.

Presentation: your dress code and professional attitude

It is important to demonstrate professional pride in your job through appropriate dress, and positive and confident language.

If your job role involves meeting customers and clients face to face, it is important that you present a clean, neat, tidy, smart, safe and practical appearance at work. Any jewellery you wear must be consistent with your organisation's Health and Safety policies and professional standards, and must not obstruct or prevent you from carrying out your duties.

Think about the following when considering your dress code:

- Is what you are wearing appropriate to your role?
- Is it likely to be viewed as offensive, revealing or sexually provocative?
- Can it cause distraction, embarrassment or give rise to misunderstanding?
- Does it have any political or otherwise contentious (controversial) slogans on it?
- Does it discriminate against anyone or is it culturally sensitive?
- Does it put you or others at risk?

While your employers shouldn't judge you on how you look, it is important to appear neat and confident in order to demonstrate that you have made an effort with your appearance. You need to dress appropriately for your trade or industry. This might mean wearing a suit and tie, or it might mean wearing specialist clothing such as overalls, aprons or another such uniform. In some creative industries, there may be a more relaxed atmosphere in which you can dress more casually.

Whatever the dress code at work, presenting yourself well shows that you have done your research and made an effort to fit in with the team. Individuality is to be commended, but you don't want to be the only person in the office wearing jeans and trainers when everyone else is smartly dressed!

Activity

Looking professional

Scenario

You are running late for work one morning and suddenly realise that you have left your work suit and smart shoes at the gym. The only ironed and presentable clothes you have are a pair of jeans, a smart/casual shirt and trainers. You are due to meet with some customers in the office that afternoon. When you arrive at work you are not completely surprised when your manager asks to see you in her office.

1. What do you think your manager will say to you?
2. What are some possible measures you could take to prevent this situation from happening again?

You have a responsibility to use professional language when dealing with customers. This means that you should follow organisational standards in both your verbal and non-verbal communication.

Remember: presentation is also an interpersonal communication skill. It is important that you are approachable when dealing with customers. Be polite, smile, make eye contact and be welcoming. Demonstrate positive language and attitude, and remain calm and focused throughout your dealings with customers.

Link

Module 8: Communication

Module 9: Interpersonal skills

Professional working

You may deal with customers in a non-face-to face situation, such as over the phone. Always use appropriate communication skills:

- **Adopt a positive tone**: When you answer the phone or call a customer, smile as you greet the person. It is well known that a smile can be heard through the phone. Smiling makes you appear welcoming and will help you to develop a rapport with the person on the other end of the line.
- **Be positive in your attitude:** Phrases such as 'How may I help you?' and 'I am sure we can deal with that' will demonstrate your willingness to help.
- **Always use professional language**: As soon as you know the caller's name, use it. Include their name naturally during the conversation. This will show that they are not just another caller and they will appreciate the personal touch.
- **Demonstrate confidence**: Be calm, even with a caller who is challenging. Remember that they have called with a problem or need help. Show them that you understand their concern and will do all you can to help.

Summary

You have seen how it is important to:

- agree deadlines to complete work
- prioritise tasks
- develop yourself using a variety of methods
- demonstrate you have good personal presentation, by dressing professionally and appropriately
- appear confident and enthusiastic in your role, and make a great first impression.

The following activities will help you strengthen the skills you have learned in this module about personal organisation.

Activities

Reflective account

List the top ten qualities you think employers are looking for. Discuss your ideas with a colleague.

EPA preparation

Make a chart of the first three things you do in the morning when you arrive at work and the last three things you do before you leave work. This will demonstrate personal organisation.

Personal development

Create an action plan showing the steps that you will need to follow. Use the following headings to create your action plan:

- Action
- Specific
- Measurable
- Agreed/Achievable
- Realistic
- Time-bound
- Who is responsible
- How to monitor

Your end-point assessment

Preparing for your end-point assessment

During your apprenticeship programme, you will undertake both on-the-job and off-the-job training. This will form part of your learning and development for the standard.

Following on from this and at least twelve months after you start, the next stage in completing your apprenticeship is to undertake the end-point assessment (EPA). You will have been working towards this with your trainer. Before moving on to this stage, your employer and training provider will meet with you to confirm you are ready and have met the gateway criteria. You and your training provider or employer will then be contacted by the external end-point assessor to plan a schedule for completing the EPA components.

You must complete all EPA components within one month from the start of your EPA assessment period. The assessment components should be completed in the order shown in the specification.

What is your end-point assessment?

The EPA is a synoptic assessment of the knowledge, skills and behaviour you have learned throughout your programme. The purpose of the EPA is to make sure you meet the standard set by employers for your given occupation so you can go on to work successfully in that field. You cannot be awarded an apprenticeship until you have successfully completed the EPA.

Your EPA is made up of an assessment plan consisting of three components. This is shown in Figure 1.

For each of the three components assessed, you must achieve all of the pass criteria in order to complete your apprenticeship.

Regardless of the number of hours allowed to complete the showcase, the last two hours of this time must be supervised. This means that you must be in the direct sight of your supervisor, who may be your trainer or tutor. You must discuss the date of this supervised period with the end-point assessor during planning and scheduling.

Throughout your programme, you will gather evidence from work activities in your portfolio as part of your apprentice showcase. This evidence will demonstrate your knowledge, skills and behaviour in your customer service role. All of this evidence will be reviewed by your trainer and employer, and you will be given feedback to assist you in your final preparation for the EPA.

Apprenticeship showcase
- Approximately 10 hours (the last two supervised)
- 65%

Practical observation
- Minimum one hour
- 20%

Professional discussion
- Maximum one hour
- 15%

Figure 1: A breakdown of the end-point assessment

Preparing your apprentice showcase

The apprentice showcase is compiled after 12 months of on-programme learning. It is a summative (combined) portfolio in which you will demonstrate, with the support of appropriate work-based evidence, how you have applied and used the identified knowledge, skills and behaviours to the required standards in your everyday work practice.

The timeframe in which you will compile your showcase is usually 10 hours, including 2 hours of supervised activity.

Your showcase will be complied against an externally-set assessment brief. This is prepared by the independent assessment organisation chosen by your employer (e.g. Edexcel) and will be assessed against the following areas in the standard:

- understanding your organisation
- meeting regulations
- following legislation
- using systems and resources
- knowing your product(s)/service(s)
- influencing skills
- personal organisation (time management)
- dealing with challenging customers and conflict
- developing yourself
- receiving feedback
- team working.

The aim is to demonstrate your knowledge and understanding of how the principles and practices of customer service work together. You will need to provide work-based evidence to demonstrate your competence (abilities) in these areas. See Figure 2 for more information.

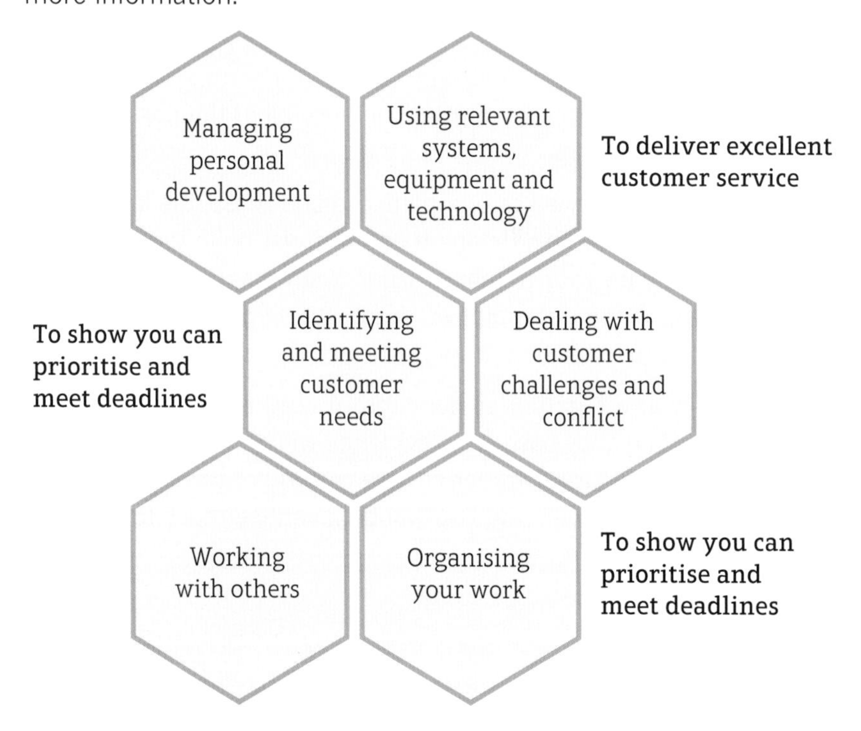

Figure 2: Areas of customer service practitioner competence

Your work-based evidence can be submitted either electronically or in hard copy format and may be all or any of the following:

- a presentation
- a report or guide
- a storyboard
- a reflective journal.

You will be guided by your trainer as to which of the above you will need to prepare. Tasks 1 and 2 can be submitted in a variety of formats but Task 3 must be a reflective account with cross-referenced descriptions, explanations and work-based evidence. See the Pearson Edexcel website https://qualifications.pearson.com/en/qualifications/new-apprenticeships/our-offer/end-point-assessment.html for the most up-to-date information.

You will draw upon evidence from your portfolio as well as any appraisal (assessment) or performance management meetings you have had at work. If you prepare a presentation and need to practice this with your trainer, you may do so during the 2 hour supervised activity.

Creating a presentation/booklet or guide

Your presentation can be in the form of slides, or even a booklet or handbook guide. It can contain relevant pictures, videos or links and may even reference your organisation's website. If relevant, you may refer to resources you use in your job such as catalogues or advertising materials.

Here are some practical tips for tackling the question 'How is customer service delivered effectively?':

1. Select the relevant material that you want to present (but check if you have been given an exact brief or tasks by the independent assessment organisation). See the Pearson Edexcel website https://qualifications.pearson.com/en/qualifications/new-apprenticeships/our-offer/end-point-assessment.html for the latest information. See Figure 3 for some examples.

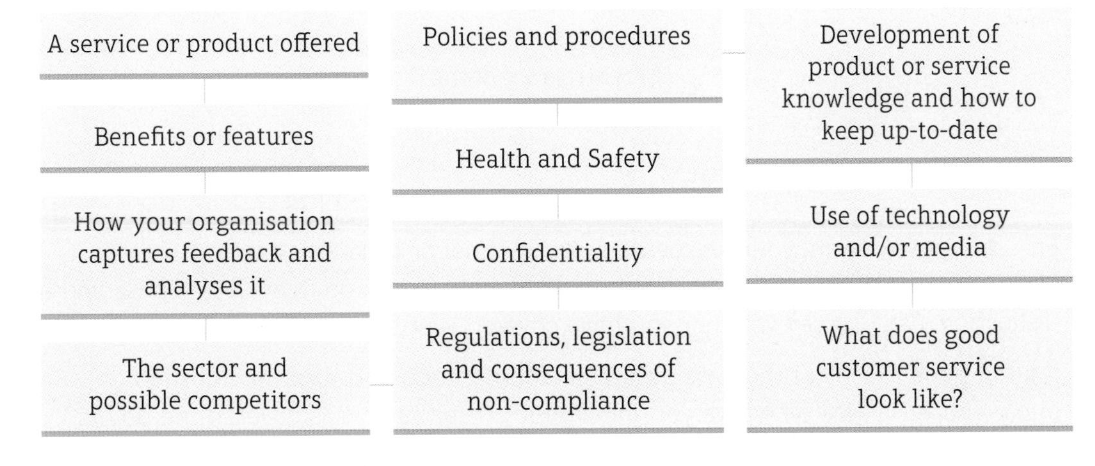

Figure 3: Examples of material to present

2. Consider the audience – they will not know you or your organisation. See Figure 4 for more information.

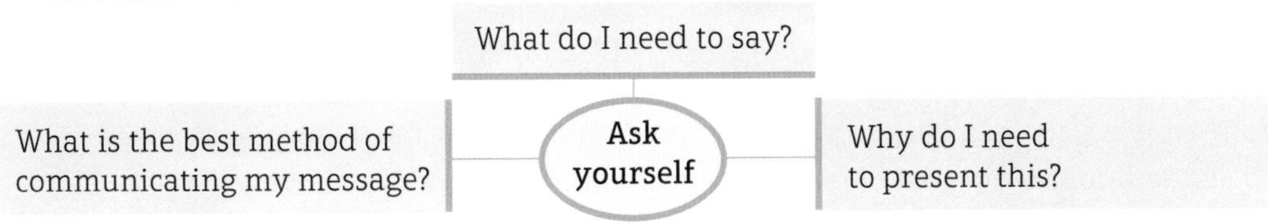

Figure 4: Key questions to ask, part 1

3. Check your material is relevant and not confidential (for example, do not use details of new product development that must not be shared outside your organisation).
4. Find out if there are any illustrations you can use.
5. Present your information in a logical sequence and structure:
   - It needs a beginning, a middle and an end.
   - If you are using slides, make sure that each slide covers one idea.
   - Do not choose too many different fonts or cram too many words onto one page. The information needs to be attractive to the eye and interesting to the reader.
   - If you are using any data and/or figures, check they will make sense to the audience.
   - Prepare your draft.
6. Practice – run through your presentation out loud.
7. Ask for feedback from others on how much they understood and how relevant your information was.
8. Edit and re-edit – take a break before you re-edit so you can look at your work with fresh eyes.
9. Spell and grammar check your work.
10. Remember to acknowledge any external references.

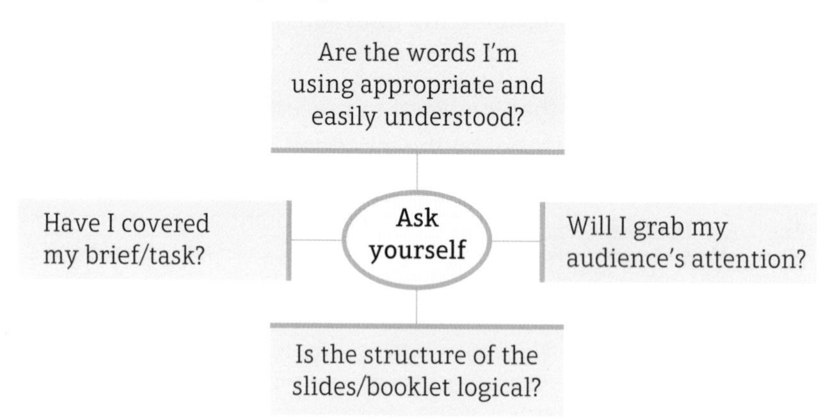

Figure 5: Key questions to ask, part 2

Ensure that you relate your presentation to any brief or tasks you have been given. Make sure you have been given details of what you need to do to achieve a pass and a distinction. Ask yourself whether you have covered everything that is expected of you.

A good tip is to look at the pass and distinction criteria and turn the information into a checklist. Tick off where you think your presentation has covered the points in the checklist.

Remember to keep the question in mind at all times: how is customer service delivered effectively?

Presenting a storyboard

You can present a storyboard as part of a PowerPoint® presentation or in a poster format. It is usually a series of pictures or diagrams that tell a story, with captions or dialogue underneath that corresponds to the picture or diagram.

Presenting a reflective journal

For your showcase, you may be asked or may choose to present a reflective journal. This will usually be based on evidence you have collected at work, such as a new procedure you introduced. Throughout this handbook, you will complete activities that will help to contribute towards your reflective journal.

A journal report will need to identify products and/or services you have offered as part of your job. It must also demonstrate your ability to handle customers and any customer service challenges effectively.

To demonstrate the skills you have learned, you will need to include evidence of self-management, self-reflection and feedback you have received from others. See Figure 6 for the reflective cycle, which you can use to help create your journal.

If relevant, you can also include audio or video clips, photographs, witness statements and work products. It must be clear to your audience what these represent and why you have included them in your journal.

In order to reflect on your work, you must describe situations that:

- were normal everyday experiences
- demonstrate that you can exceed a customer's expectations
- show how you have communicated and influenced your customers.

Think about any challenges you have had, what you have learned from your experience and how you have managed your own personal development.

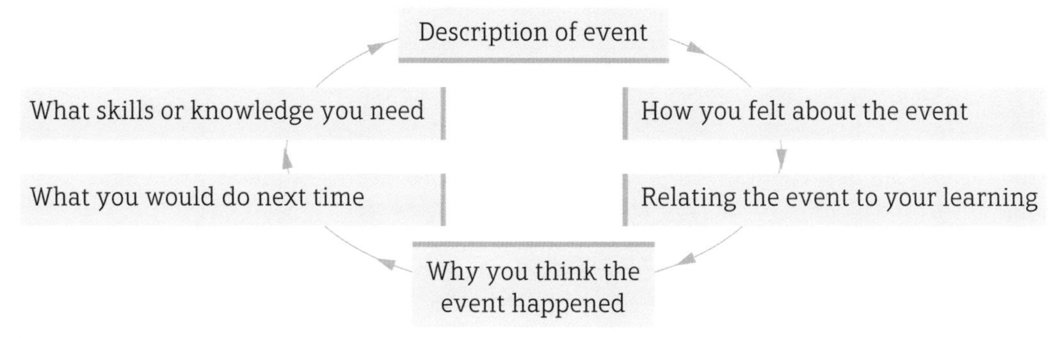

Figure 6: You can use the reflective cycle to help you reflect on your work

Here are some tips for thinking about what to include in your journal:

- Try to make sense of an event or customer objection. What did this teach you?
- What knowledge helped you to manage a situation?
- Look at a particular process or procedure your organisation uses. Did you work with others on this? Does it work or does it need revision?
- What went well and what did not go so well? What would you do differently next time?
- How did you feel about an experience?
- Share your ideas or learning with others.

Your trainer will help you to make this into a checklist so you can tick off where you think your journal has covered particular skills and/or behaviour.

Remember to keep the question in mind at all times – how is customer service delivered effectively?

Practical observation

The observation will happen at your place of work. During the observation you will be judged on:

- how you present yourself – your behaviour in the workplace
- your communication and interpersonal skills with internal and external customers
- whether you treat customers fairly and your knowledge of your role within your organisation
- your personal organisational skills.

Link 

Modules 1, 2, 3, 6, 7: Equality and diversity

Preparing for your observation

Your practical observation will take place at a time that falls within your normal working hours. It will be agreed with your trainer, employer and the independent assessor. You will be given support to prepare and plan for this activity. You will also be given details of the criteria against which you will be judged. These will link to the knowledge, skills and behaviours you covered in your apprenticeship programme of learning.

You will already have been observed by your trainer on several occasions during your programme. On these occasions, you should have demonstrated your knowledge, skills and how you behave in the workplace. The formal observation may be similar to the example below.

Scenario

You have to phone a client to tell them that your boss, Mr Keene, is unable to keep his appointment as he will be on jury service. You must make clear to your client that this is an unavoidable situation (adapt your tone, language and interpersonal skills to interact effectively and employ active listening skills). Mr Keene has suggested that his colleague, Miss Salisbury, could meet with the client instead as he has fully briefed her (offer a workable option to your client and explain the reasons clearly and politely, remaining calm if the client gets annoyed). The client may need reassurance before agreeing (listen and influence). Ensure that you agree the solution (confirm the actions agreed with both the client and Miss Salisbury).

Here are some tips for approaching the practical observation:

- act and work as you would normally – you will have had observations by your trainer or employer already so try not to be nervous
- speak slowly and clearly to your customers and use active listening skills
- review any feedback given by your trainer after they observed you at work to remind yourself what you did well and what needed improving
- practise using words and phrases that promote your good customer service skills – avoid slang and jargon.

Link 

Module 6: Knowing your customers

Module 8: Communication

Professional discussion

Your professional discussion will be pre-planned with your employer and the independent assessor, just like the observation. It is likely to follow the observation. It may take place immediately, in which case it will happen at your workplace, or at another location on an agreed date. It may also be recorded for clarification purposes. The aim is to explore more about your work, for example how you follow procedures and carry out tasks.

Preparing for your professional discussion

Your professional discussion is likely to be used to clarify points and raise any additional questions arising from your observation or any submitted written work, such as your reflective journal. The independent assessor may also use it to explore a 'what if' scenario. This would cover something that did not occur in your observation but that the assessor is keen to ask you about in order to explore how you would deal with it. You will be asked to discuss your personal development and reflections on your last year at work. This may also require you to reference your quality of service.

You will be asked a series of focused questions. The end-point assessor will guide the discussion, asking you to provide real-work examples of how you applied the knowledge you gained during your apprenticeship.

Example questions might include the following:

- Explain the difference between internal and external customers, and the ways in which these relationships are managed.
- Explain the importance to your organisation of building good customer relationships and give an example of when you have done this.
- Describe or give an example of when you have met specific needs of customers protected under current equality law.
- Give an example of when you had to adapt your approach to a customer in order to meet their needs and expectations, and why it was important to balance both their needs and that of your organisation.
- Explain how your understanding of the facts of, for example, a complaint enabled you to create a customer-focused experience.
- Explain how you build trust with customers and why this is important.

Remember that your showcase relates to work you have done as an apprentice in your job. The professional discussion may focus on this or something that is in your portfolio.

Here are some tips for approaching the professional discussion:

- Speak slowly and clearly – do not interrupt or talk over the other person.
- Review your portfolio to remind yourself of the evidence and events that you recorded so that you can locate them if asked.
- Be mindful of confidentiality and GDPR when providing real work examples – you will cover the importance of these things during your programme of learning. Note that you must not give away confidential details – for example a new product launch – or give a client's real name. Always anonymise any evidence that you use.
- Listen to questions and do not be afraid to ask for something to be repeated if you do not hear or understand – do not let your attention drift.
- Avoid jargon or acronyms that are specific to your organisation – your listener may not understand or be familiar with these terms.
- Be specific and as detailed as possible when discussing your example(s).
- Ask yourself questions as you listen in case you need to clarify any points.
- Take notes if this helps you – you might need to revisit a point.
- Be confident – you have done really well to get to this stage.

Glossary

AbilityNet – free helpline providing advice and information for disabled people on the use of computers and the internet.

ACAS – The Advisory, Conciliation and Arbitration Service is a government body that provides advice to employers and employees on all aspects of employment rights.

Aim – something you want to achieve (an intention).

Assertiveness – clear and direct communication – being assertive allows you to state what you want and to say 'no' firmly without causing offence.

Benefits – how a product or service helps someone.

Bespoke – something designed specifically for you, or for an organisation.

Biased – **(1)** having a preference for a purpose or thing, and favouring that person or thing.

(2) when someone or something is unfairly prejudiced in a certain direction.

Bottom line – how much money the company makes.

Brand – a type of product created by a particular organisation under a particular name and usually unique to them in some way.

Buddy – someone who supports you at work and provides advice.

Code of professional conduct – a list of company standards that staff should follow when dealing with vendors, customers and employees.

Codes of practice – written guidelines on how you should behave in your organisation.

Colleague – someone in your team who works alongside you.

Commercially – in a way that focuses on buying, selling and making a profit.

Complaint – when a customer contacts an organisation to complain about its goods or services. Customer service organisations work hard to meet customer expectations.

Concession – offering an allowance, special rate or gift to compensate for a faulty product or poor service.

Contract of employment – this forms the agreement between employer (your organisation) and employee (you). It helps you understand what employers expect of you during your employment with them. It outlines the terms and conditions that you agree to, for example hours of work, location, duties, time off, sick pay, holidays, confidentiality agreement, IT policy and termination of contract conditions.

Convert a lead – the process of changing a new contact into a lead or an opportunity for a sale. In a call centre, customer service practitioners will have targets for converting leads into new accounts, and must then promote features and benefits to the customer in order to achieve a sale.

Copyright – protects the creator of a piece of work (which could be creative work or work produced during work time).

Customer portal access – allows customers to set up their own access to your organisation, for example to a recruitment area.

e-books – books that are in an electronic rather than paper format so they can be downloaded onto a computer.

Empathising – being able to share and understand others' feelings – you may, for example, have experienced the same scenario or situation.

Equality – maintaining fairness of opportunity with regard to jobs, pay and promotion.

Equipment, machinery and plant – this refers to the land, buildings, office equipment, vehicles (cars, trucks, forklift machinery), furniture and so on used by organisations to carry out their day-to-day business.

e-reader – a hand-held reading device that allows multiple books and films to be downloaded for viewing.

Ethical standards – principles that promote trust and fair behaviour.

Features – the important parts of a product.

Front of house – customer service practitioners who meet and greet customers, or who are the first point of contact for customers who send emails or call with a query.

Generic – a general product or brand with no copyright or trademark that is available for anyone to use.

Goal – an aim or desired result.

Goods warranty – a written statement issued by your organisation or a product's manufacturer that promises to repair or replace an item within a certain period of time after purchase.

Health and Safety Executive (HSE) – a group that is responsible for managing health, safety and risk management in the workplace. It provides guidance, posters, templates and literature relating to health and safety for employees and employers.

Hierarchy chart (organogram) – shows the reporting lines in a team, department or organisation and how the job roles relate to each other.

Impartial – treating everyone equally and without bias; not being too involved in a situation.

Incentive – something to provide motivation to do better.

Influencing – being able to affect or change how someone or something develops, behaves, or thinks (a combination of persuading and negotiating).

Invoice – a bill itemising how much money is owed to an individual or organisation.

Jargon – special words or expressions that may be difficult for others to understand.

Job boards – online recruitment sites providing details of available jobs.

Line manager – the person you report to at work.

Live chat room – a venue in which people can chat about their common interests online.

Loan or hire agreement – an agreement between two parties who decide on terms and conditions for the purchase of goods or services.

Mission statement – a written summary of an organisation's aims, goals and values.

Mystery shoppers – people who measure the quality of service, or gather specific information about a product or service for an organisation.

Negotiating – being able to discuss and reach a mutually satisfactory agreement.

Non-compliance – failing to comply with (act on) a rule, regulation or law.

Objective – something that is aimed for; a goal.

Overheads – the running costs of a business (taxes, lighting, heating, etc.).

Paraphrase – to reword something (either written or spoken) in order to make it clearer.

Persuading – being able to convince others to take appropriate action(s).

Point of sale (POS) – combines software and hardware systems to take payment from customers for products or services.

Priority – something that is more important than another.

Proactive – taking control and moving a situation forward before an issue occurs rather than dealing with a situation after it has happened.

Probation – an initial period of time in which to see how a new employee fits into the organisation. The period can be extended if an employer is not sure how suitable the person is. Employees are only required to give one week's notice when in a probation period.

Product – an item that is offered for sale at a cost.

Professional body – a not-for-profit group that oversees and regulates a particular profession, providing advice and support.

Profit – a financial benefit to a business that occur when the amount of income generated is higher than the combined cost and expenses of running the business.

Protocol – unwritten rules, or guidelines, that should be followed in business dealings, and are usually learned in on-the-job training.

QR code – a quick response (QR) code is a barcode containing information that can be read by smartphones; you scan the QR code in a book or product and then watch a linked video on your phone.

Qualitative – often expressed as an opinion or type using our senses.

Quantitative – data that you can count, usually expressed in numbers.

Rapport – a relationship between two or more people in which each person understands the other and everyone communicates well.

Revenue stream – a business term meaning sales or income.

Satisfactory quality – products or services must be of a 'satisfactory' standard for the consumer to want to purchase them.

Segmentation – dividing your customers into groups to identify their specific needs – this is especially useful for marketing purposes.

Self-service points – customers can scan and pay for items at a point of sale without the need for a member of staff.

Service – a system, such as a transport or communications service, or the act of helping or working for someone.

Service culture – organisations with an effective service culture train and reward staff that put the customer first.

Service standards – these define what a customer can expect and provide guidance to employees about the level of work they are expected to produce.

Service users – individuals using health and social services.

Shareholders – individuals or organisations who invest in a business by buying shares; shareholders are entitled to voting rights in appointing governors to a board of directors.

Skills audit – a process in which you check and list your skills.

Smart connectivity – where non-computers detect and analyse customer data, for example a refrigerator that recognises when you are low on food items, or a stapler that recognises when you are low on staples. Sensors are embedded into software applications allowing data exchange between the product and the manufacturer.

SMART targets – this stands for Simple, Measurable, Accurate, Realistic and Timely, and is a guide to setting objectives.

Social responsibility – the practice of producing goods and services that are not harmful to society.

Sole trader – a business that is set up and controlled by one person; they take all the risk and profit relating to the business.

Staff charter – document designed to provide staff with clarity and a shared understanding of what is expected at work, in order to ensure that they deliver high quality service to all customers.

Sue – to take legal action against an individual or organisation.

Suppliers – businesses work with external organisations who provide products or services at a cost to the business.

Support ticketing – a service request from an end user asking for support.

Sustainability – managing natural resources so they are maintained for future need.

Target – an objective to work towards.

Taxes – compulsory sums of money paid by businesses to the government; a business pays different types of tax, such as value-added tax (VAT) or employment tax.

Telecommunications technology – exchanging information using technology.

Telephony system – a system for making calls over the internet using computer software, hardware and network systems that provide the functions of a traditional telephone system. It is cheaper to run and can be used from any location with a computer and an internet connection. A traditional landline connects calls between two phones, limiting its use in larger organisations.

Trading standards officer – people who advise consumers and businesses about legislation relating to the buying, selling and hiring of goods and services.

Transparency – being open and honest about your activities.

Up-selling – encouraging the customer to buy something more expensive or in addition to the original sale, for example offering a customer a book of stamps if they buy envelopes, or a scented body lotion to complement a bottle of perfume.

Urgent – something that needs immediate attention.

Warranty (or guarantee) – a written contract provided to the purchaser that promises to repair or replace an item within a given timeframe.

Web page – these promote an organisation online and lead the customer to the information required.

Index